Why Read
Four Quartets?

Why Read
Four Quartets?

Tom Brous

RESOURCE *Publications* · Eugene, Oregon

WHY READ *FOUR QUARTETS?*

Resource Publications
An Imprint of Wipf and Stock Publishers
199 W. 8th Ave., Suite 3
Eugene, OR 97401

www.wipfandstock.com

PAPERBACK ISBN: 978-1-5326-3568-7
HARDCOVER ISBN: 978-1-5326-3570-0
EBOOK ISBN: 978-1-5326-3569-4

Manufactured in the U.S.A.   SEPTEMBER 28, 2017

Contents

Introduction | *vii*

Chapter 1   Spiritual Journey | 1

Chapter 2   Another Spiritual Journey | 6

Chapter 3   Literary Tourism | 12

Chapter 4   Divine Geometry | 25

Chapter 5   Mysticism | 31

Chapter 6   Krishna | 44

Chapter 7   Dante | 50

Chapter 8   The Journey Began | 58

Chapter 9   Puritans Against Arminians | 83

Chapter 10   Lent | 93

Chapter 11   Love Story | 99

Appendix | *101*

Bibliography | *103*

Introduction

O ver thirty years ago I read T. S. Eliot's *Four Quartets* for the first time. It was not at all clear to me what I had read due to the complexity of ideas and unfamiliar references. Trying to understand the meaning of the four poems became a challenge— and eventually a passion—for me, and that passion continues to this day. These poems, like any great work of art, grow on you with each reading, which without exception brings new insights into the meaning. My hope in writing this small book is to encourage readers unfamiliar with *Four Quartets* to "take up, read and inwardly digest" (in the words of *The Book of Common Prayer)* these precious and, indeed, sacred poems.

A significant reason for my passion for these poems is that their study over the years led me on a spiritual journey of my own. As explained in Chapter 1 ("Spiritual Journey") my reading of these poems, as well as Eliot's other post-1927 writings represent Eliot's own spiritual journey (in 1927 Eliot joined the Anglican Church and these later works are often referred to as "post-conversion" works). Thus, Eliot's journey in his writings became a guide, a roadmap, for my own journey. A disclaimer—this book is not intended in any way to be a scholarly treatise on *Four Quartets*. I am no academic. Moreover, the scholarly treatment of Eliot's spiritual journey has been ably addressed by Professor G. Douglas Atkins in his recent book, *Reading T. S. Eliot/Four Quartets and The Journey Toward Understanding* (2012). Instead, my book is based on my experience, my journey, with the Quartets.

A major part of the altogether consuming experience I have had with the Quartets was the unexpected introduction to other authors whose work supports the text of the Quartets, and more importantly whose work I might otherwise never have read. For example, Dante (*The Divine Comedy*), John of the Cross (*The Ascent of Mount Camel and The Dark Night*), and Dame Julian of Norwich (*Revelations of Divine Love*), in addition to *The Cloud of Unknowing* and *The Bhagavad Gita*, whose authors are unknown. It really is not an overstatement to say if all the references and allusions in *Four Quartets* are traced to their source documents and studied, a post-graduate equivalent education would be provided to the reader. And that presents somewhat of a quandary for me—I had such a wonderful time reading these many books, I hope that this book's summary treatment of these works will not deter anyone from reading the source texts themselves.

There must be an acknowledgement to Nathaniel Philbrick and his book, *Why Read Moby-Dick?*, published in 2011. Obviously, his title has been appropriated. Much more importantly, however, is the inspiration Mr. Philbrick provided to me to try to get you, the reader, to read *Four Quartets*, whether it be for the first time or the twentieth. To paraphrase Mr. Philbrick—read a sentence in the Quartets ("The hint half guessed, the gift half understood, is Incarnation."), a mere phrase will do ("At the still point"). The important thing is to spend time with the poems, to listen as you read, to feel the poetry adapt to the various voices that flowed through Eliot as he wrote the poems like "intermittent ghosts with something urgent and essential to say."

Each chapter in this book suggests a good reason for reading *Four Quartets.* Those reasons are:

- story of Eliot's own spiritual journey
- may remind of your own spiritual journey
- invites visits to sites which inspired Eliot to write

- learn about the "still point"
- learn about mysticism
- invites you to read *The Bhagavad Gita*
- invites you to read *The Divine Comedy*
- see how *Four Quartets* was influenced by Eliot's earlier poetry
- provides daily readings for Lent
- meet heretofore unknown 17th-century Englishmen and women

As Eliot himself often said, you do not necessarily have to understand the poetry to enjoy it. Since the four poems are not linear and certainly not sequential, there is no need to begin with "Burnt Norton," the first poem, and read through to the end of "Little Gidding," the final poem. Begin anywhere. Simply pick up and read. I think you will be amazed at what you will find.

Chapter 1

Spiritual Journey

In spite of the fact that *Four Quartets* provides an account of a spiritual journey, the question I have always asked myself is: Do the poems represent Eliot's own spiritual journey? Not surprisingly, critics disagree about the answer to that question. Let's examine one critic on each side of the issue, as well as Eliot's own position on the abstract question of whether poetry can ever be linked to the poet's own life.

Eliot was very clear on the answer to that question in 1920 in his essay, "Tradition and the Individual Talent," which was published in his volume of essays entitled *The Sacred Wood and Major Early Essays.* In this essay, Eliot set forth his "Impersonal theory of poetry" which posits that poetry "is not the expression of personality, but an escape from personality."[1] The personality referred to, of course, is that of the poet. So there would be no misunderstanding, Eliot repeats: "the progress of an artist is a continual self-sacrifice, a continual extinction of personality."[2] Finally, Eliot writes: "the more perfect the artist, the more completely separate in him will be the man who suffers and the mind which creates . . . "[3] Thesewords were written in 1920, and in my view Eliot's spiritual journey as

1. Eliot, *The Sacred Wood and Major Early Essays*, 33.
2. Ibid., 30.
3. Ibid., 31.

reflected in his poetry really does not commence until his baptism and confirmation in the Church of England in 1927, so perhaps he changed his mind about impersonality.

There is indeed some evidence Eliot did later change his mind about impersonality. In a letter dated August 10, 1929, from Eliot to E. M. Forster, Eliot wrote: "As for the 'impersonality' doctrine, it has its personal motives of course, and neither more true nor more false than the opposite doctrine; but I believe that it may have been of some value in its time."[4] Later in his 1940 essay "Yeats," Eliot wrote:

> I have, in early essays, extolled what I called impersonality in art, and it may seem that, in giving as a reason for the superiority of Yeats's later work the greater expression of personality in it, I am contradicting myself. It may be that I expressed myself badly, or that I had only an adolescent grasp of that idea—as I can never bear to re-read my own prose writings, I am willing to leave the point unsettled—but I think now, at least, that the truth of the matter is as follows . . . [5]

He then goes on to explain there are two forms of impersonality, one that is natural to the author and one that is achieved by the "mature artist." Several of Eliot's friends had a nickname of "Old Possum" for him because he was known as a trickster who did not always say what he really meant. Perhaps the impersonality doctrine was Old Possum's way of misleading his readers.

Taking the position that *Four Quartets* should not be read as spiritual biography, Craig Raine, in his book, *T.S. Eliot*, argues that it is difficult "to equate biographical events with the poetry."[6] Eliot himself, as we saw above, argued for "impersonality" in a writer's work. Raine accepts Eliot's assertion of the impersonality of great art and concludes "aesthetic distance means it is dangerous and difficult to translate the poetry . . . back into personal experience."[7] Nevertheless, there is in any art, Raine concedes, a personal element which

4. Eliot and Haffenden, *The Letters of T. S. Eliot, Vol.* 4, 573.

5. Eliot, "Yeats," lines 134–41.

6. Raine, *T. S. Eliot*, xv.

7. Ibid., xvii.

derives from the poet's own emotions. The poet's own emotions became the components that are made into the work of art.

On the other hand, there is G. Douglas Atkins who writes in his recent book about *Four Quartets, T.S. Eliot and the Fulfillment of Christian Poetics*, "Eliot's words bear greater relevance to his own journey toward belief than is, I believe, often recognized."[8] Earlier in his *Reading T.S. Eliot/Four Quarters and the Journey Toward Understanding*, Atkins had written, "Eliot's own 'path' or progress was itself a journey to understanding, visable in the poems and essays and mirroring the sequence he posits."[9]

My view is that *Four Quartets* is Eliot's spiritual biography. What has been called the greatest religious poetry of the twentieth century and possibly since Dante's *The Divine Comedy* surely must have sprung from Eliot's own personal experience. To say he was writing "impersonally" strains credulity. He was on record as saying the poems were about the experience of believing the dogma of the Incarnation, and that dogma held central importance to Eliot's writing, beginning with the first *Ariel Poem* ('Journey of the Magi') in 1927, and continuing in *Ash Wednesday*, *The Rock*, and *Murder in the Cathedral*. Incarnation is never far from Eliot's attention. Moreover, the favorite authors he read wrote about their own spiritual journeys in such works—*The Divine Comedy*, *The Ascent of Mount Carmel/The Dark Night*, *The Cloud of Unknowing*, *Revelations of Divine Love*, and *The Bhagavad Gita*.

Of all these examples, *The Divine Comedy* was probably the most significant to Eliot. In his 1929 essay on Dante, Eliot wrote: "The majority of poems one outgrows and outlives, as one outgrows and outlives the majority of human passions: Dante's is one of those which can only just hope to grow up to at the end of life."[10] He called the last canto of *Paradiso* "the highest point that poetry has ever reached or ever can reach."[11]

---

8. Atkins, *T. S. Eliot and the Fulfillment of Christian Poetics*, 4.

9. Atkins, *Reading T. S. Eliot*, viii.

10. Eliot, *Selected Essays*, 251.

11. Ibid., 251.

If we accept for the moment that *Four Quartets* is Eliot's spiritual biography, then I want to speculate on why Eliot ceased publishing any major poetry after 1942, when "Little Gidding" was first published (Although it is hardly major, there seems to be only one poem even published after 1942 until his death in 1965—a final *Ariel Poem*, "The Cultivation of Christmas Trees" [1954]). The poetry may have stopped because Eliot seemed to have abandoned his spiritual journey. Lyndall Gordon concluded that Eliot in 1942 accepted "the fact he was not a candidate for the divine spirit."[12] Gordon explains: "Eliot's journey, though, ends where it began. Its final form is circular. After the effort at transformation, Eliot realizes that he has become what was always implicit in his origins . . . he has not changed."[13] His life suggests he aspired to complete the mystical journey to union with the Divine, but in the end did not have the vocation of a mystic. Paraphrasing Ms. Gordon, he reached for but could not attain reconciliation of pain and divine love. There may have been an inability to accept forgiveness ("the rendering pain of re-enactment / Of all that you have done, and been; the shame / Of motives late revealed, and the awareness / Of things ill done and done to others' harm / Which once you took for exercise of virtue.").[14]

Carrying my speculation further, there is an interesting "what if?" Ms. Gordon writes that in the 1950s Eliot read the Harvard theologian Paul Tillich, and in particular his *Systematic Theology* (1951–1963). Tillich argued that forgiveness does not come from anything we do—not self-accusation or self-rejection ("There is no condition whatsoever in man which would make him worthy of forgiveness.").[15] There is no condition in man justifying forgiveness, except man's need for it. Instead, "[f]orgiveness is an answer, the divine answer, to the question implied in our existence."[16] In 1955 Tillich published a book of his sermons, *The New Being*, in

12. Gordon, *T. S. Eliot*, 385.
13. Ibid., 388.
14. Eliot, *Collected Poems*, 204.
15. Tillich, *New Being*, 12–13.
16. Ibid., 9.

which he said, "In the midst of our futile attempts to make ourselves worthy, in our despair about the inescapable failure of these attempts, we are suddenly grasped by the certainty that we are forgiven, and the fire of love begins to burn."[17]

That love seemed to begin to burn in Eliot when he married Valerie Fletcher, his secretary for many years, on January 10, 1957. Ms. Gordon writes that "in 1956, there appeared the possibility of a different pattern of redemption: not through the heights of divine communion—those heights of the mystics were now closed to Eliot—but through a human solace."[18] That human solace being Eliot's new wife. From that point on until his death in 1965, Eliot seemed happier that he had ever been in his entire life; he was in Tillich's terms a "new being."

What if Eliot had read Tillich earlier; say in 1943? Would he have been able to accept forgiveness and continue his spiritual journey? Would the poetry have continued to be written? I like to dream about the possibility of more great poetry if his spiritual journey had only continued in his final years.

Since Old Possum was extremely coy as to whether the poetry was indeed his spiritual biography, we shall never know for sure whether *Four Quartets* is or is not. In the end however, it probably makes no difference because what Eliot has given us is amazing poetry which describes what a spiritual journey could very well look like. Eliot's loss if he did abandon the journey is nevertheless still our great gain. As Ms. Gordon has written that Eliot, "wished to be a saint above poet, but who became all the greater poet for his failure to attain sainthood."[19]

17. Ibid., 9.
18. Gordon, *T. S. Eliot*, 520.
19. Ibid., 535.

Chapter 2

Another Spiritual Journey

Bidden or not bidden / God is present

—WORDS ON TOMBSTONE OF CARL JUNG

For over thirty years, T.S. Eliot's *Four Quartets* has been a guide for my own spiritual journey. The epigraph from Carl Jung's tombstone quoted above states the prerequisite for any journey to the Divine—whether we recognize the Divine or not in our own life, the Divine is nevertheless present. The truly remarkable offering of *Four Quartets* is the affirmation of the continual presence ("Bidden or not bidden") and accessibility of the Divine in the present in a suffering world. In other words, we can experience incarnation. We can see the intersection of the Divine with our own individual lives. As the poems so eloquently suggest, we need only be looking for incarnation.

In the early 1980s, I attended a lecture by Morton Kelsey—theologian, psychologist, Episcopal priest, and educator (former professor at Notre Dame University)—in which he discussed his book *The Other Side of Silence*. He talked about meditation and how stillness and silence could deepen your spiritual life. Stillness and silence seemed totally foreign to me, having grown up in a

Southern Baptist tradition where spirituality seemed focused entirely on reading the Bible. Since I was intrigued, my recreational reading quickly shifted from history (the American Civil War was a particular interest) to silence and contemplative prayer. At some point I read *The Still Point: Reflections on Zen and Christian Mysticism* by William Johnston, SJ, an Irish priest who taught at Sophia University in Tokyo. Not surprising to any reader of *Four Quartets* (but upon my initial reading the term "still point" was unknown to me), the title of Johnston's book alone was a giveaway that the book would have something to say about Eliot's *Four Quartets*. The poems were abstruse and held little meaning for me on the first reading. I did sense however that something exciting, wonderful, possibly even sacred, was contained in the poems—if only the poems could be decoded. I was challenged to gain an understanding of the Quartets. And so began my spiritual journey with Eliot as my guide (can I be so bold as to say Eliot was my Virgil as Virgil had been Dante's guide in his journey to the Divine?).

My journey began much like a game of hopscotch—moving indirectly and making many stops with different authors whose works influenced Eliot in his writing of *Four Quartets*. I jumped around from John of the Cross to Dante to Evelyn Underhill to Augustine and so on.

Recalling that early reading program, I am reminded of a particular night spent reading John of the Cross's *The Ascent of Mount Carmel* in a bus depot in Goodland, Kansas. The year in question was 1976 because I remember the Olympics being on the television set in our motel room. My family was spending the night midway on its drive between Kansas City and Breckenridge, Colorado. Soon after checking into the motel my five-year-old son managed to break the door key off in the lock of our car's door. Of course we carried no spare key. The car we drove was an Audi, and no one we contacted in this small Kansas town seemed to have ever heard of the brand or whether there was a locksmith who could deal with a foreign car. The only solution which came to mind was to call my father in Kansas City, have him go to our house to retrieve a spare set of keys, and put the keys on a Greyhound bus arriving in

Goodland at 3 a.m. later that evening. The bus station was several miles from the motel. There were no taxi cabs. The motel manager recommended calling the local sheriff when I wished to go to the bus depot in the middle of the night. Not wanting to test that means of transport, and being unwilling to walk the two to three miles to the bus depot in the middle of the night, I decided to walk into the town in the early evening while there was still daylight. The bus depot was actually the town's hotel. Arriving about 8 p.m. I spent the next seven hours reading *The Ascent of Mount Carmel*, which as I recall was the only book I had taken with me to read on the vacation. Perhaps I should have been reading John of the Cross's companion volume, *The Dark Night*, instead because it was indeed a very lonely, dark night sitting and reading in a deserted bus depot. The bus did arrive with the keys, and the driver was kind enough to give me a ride back to the motel.

Before the story proceeds too far with the reading of spiritual classics, let me circle back to the beginning in order to describe my earlier years. I grew up in a family which attended a Southern Baptist Church. Weekly church attendance was intense—four times on Sunday (Sunday school, morning worship, Baptist Training Union at 6 o'clock, and evening worship) and back again on Wednesday evening for a potluck supper and a prayer meeting. I discovered the particular church we attended was more progressive than other churches in the denomination when I attended a statewide church camp in the Ozarks. At the camp, card-playing, dominoes, and other games were strictly prohibited. Of course, there was no dancing even though all the campers were teenagers (who were most likely doing plenty of dancing back home). Swimming was strictly segregated by gender. Back at my home church, however, there were none of these taboos against games, dancing, and boys/girls swimming together—or adults drinking alcohol for that matter, if little was said about the subject.

Over my high school years however, I became increasingly uncomfortable with the extreme informality of the church services. I recall one worship service when the phone rang in the sanctuary (why there was a phone installed there I never understood) during the sermon, and the pastor said "would somebody please answer the phone?" and the pastor halted his sermon while the ringing phone was answered. So I was primed to move on to a different style of worship, and what I found at the University Chapel at Northwestern University was a more formal, liturgical style of service. *The Book of Common Prayer* was used for the order of worship. From time to time I attended the local Episcopal church as well. In both venues I found new church homes. The formality, order of worship, gothic architecture, and music totally displaced whatever Southern Baptist spirituality was left in my bones.

During my undergraduate studies at Northwestern University, I took a number of courses in the History and Literature of Religions Department, including both Old and New Testaments. The University Chapel was itself organized as a congregation known as the University Chapel Association, and I served one year as president of the organization.

Moving on to law school at the University of Michigan, I was confirmed in the Episcopal Church at St. Andrews Church in Ann Arbor. The confirmation process was vigorous—meeting for several hours with the rector every Sunday evening for six months leading up to confirmation. After returning to Kansas City, I joined another St. Andrews church and served on the vestry, as a lay Eucharistic minister serving communion during the service, and afterwards taking communion to ill persons at home. For many years I served as the chancellor of Grace and Holy Trinity Cathedral ("chancellor" is just a fancy name for the church's legal counsel).

During the 1970s I participated in two activities which were formative for my spiritual journey—Cursillo and the Bethel Bible Series. The Cursillo Movement has a number of components; the entry point is a four-day weekend (Thursday evening to Sunday evening) spent listening to fifteen talks given by clergy and lay persons about the fundamentals of Christian faith (hence it is known as a short course on Christianity). During the seventy-two hours, "candidates" (those persons attending the weekend for the first time) and "team" (those who have previously attended a weekend and then organize, present, and provide all arrangements, including meals) live typically within the confines of a church building of a parish willing to host a Cursillo weekend. Following the weekend, small groups (four to five people) meet weekly in a so-called Group Reunion to discuss and renew the ideas presented in the weekend talks. Once a month the separate Group Reunions in an area join together for a meeting known as an *Ultreya* (a Spanish word meaning "onward"). The Cursillo Movement began in Majorca in 1944 by Roman Catholic laymen, and has since spread to other denominations, including Episcopal, Lutheran, and Presbyterian.

The Bethel Bible Series is an intensive study of the Old and New Testaments. The teacher training required twenty weekly classes each year for two years—studying the Old Testament during the first year and the New Testament the next year. Following the two years of teacher training, I then taught my own class of approximately twenty people over the next two years. My continuing love of teaching probably grew out of the experience of teaching the Bethel classes.

For many years different forms of meditation have been part of my practice. Initially, I used (and still do) the so-called Jesus Prayer ("Lord Jesus Christ, son of God, have mercy on me") as described in *The Way of a Pilgrim*, a story of a nineteenth-century mendicant pilgrim walking across Russia while constantly reciting this prayer. More recently, my wife and I practice "Centering Prayer," which is most closely associated with Father Thomas Keating, a Benedictine monk who lives at St. Benedict's Monastery in Snowmass, Colorado. For my sixtieth birthday my wife surprised me with a three-day retreat at the monastery. We stayed in a small cabin and arose at 4:30 a.m. to attend the first and second services in the Daily Office. In the evening we attended Vespers, but the other services in the monks' day were not open to visitors. We did see Father Keating, but were not able to speak with him. The method of Centering Prayer is to sit for a twenty-minute period and try to dismiss any thought, idea, or image which might come to mind while sitting in silence. When any of these do intrude, you silently repeat a chosen word or concentrate on your breath in order to dismiss the intruder and return to not thinking about anything—trying to make your mind blank so that other issues deep inside may come to the surface.

Soon after embarking on my reading program of the works supporting the Quartets, I wanted to share these great poems with others. I developed a series of one-hour lectures on each Quartet and presented the lectures to adult education programs at several churches. As I expanded my reading to all Eliot's post-conversion writings, I came to see all of his post-1927 poetry and plays (*Ariel Poems, Ash Wednesday, The Rock, Murder in the Cathedral* and *The Family Reunion*) to be parts of a very integrated spiritual journey—if not for Eliot personally, then certainly for me. Presentations on the post-1927 works were developed and presented to church groups, as well as other groups including the Kansas City chapter of Friends of Carl Jung.

For many years it has been my intention to write a book based on those lectures with the purpose of trying to motivate anyone who has not read *Four Quartets* to take up and read. In late 2014, I was diagnosed with lymphoma and forced to take a medical leave of absence from practicing law. This illness has thus provided an opportunity for me to reflect on my journey with the Quartets and the other writings, and offer my thoughts as to why one should read *Four Quartets.*

We live in a suffering world. A world where war and violence are daily experiences for many people, and many live with illness. These poems present the case that even in a suffering world there is the continual presence, and more importantly I believe, the accessibility of the Divine in the present. Incarnation can be experienced. The Divine is present in the world. "And all shall be well and / All manner of thing shall be well."[1]

---

1. Eliot, *Collected Poems,* 209.

Chapter 3

Literary Tourism

L iterary tourism is the practice of visiting sites related to works of literature and their authors. It is not a recent practice at all, having been practiced for several centuries, especially in the nineteenth century. Typically the homes, graves, and haunts of famous authors are visited as well as the sites described in the works of the authors of interest. By visiting such sites the reader may experience what he or she has read in a more meaningful way, and indeed the reading experience may come alive in a completely new way. Moreover, by seeing the site that inspired the author the reader may gain a better understanding of the impact of the site on the author's inspiration.

Given the spiritual nature of *Four Quartets*, any visitation to the specific sites referenced in these poems should be called a spiritual pilgrimage instead. To visit the chapel at Little Gidding ("where prayer has been valid") brings alive to the reader the spiritual emotion of what the poet surely felt when he visited the chapel in 1936. Likewise, a visit to the Rose Garden at Burnt Norton brings a new and greater understanding of the awakening experience described in the poem based on an actual visit by Eliot and Emily Hale in 1934. Only by actually being on the ground can a full appreciation of what the site meant to the author be appreciated by the reader.

For our first ten years together, my wife and I talked about making a journey to each of the four sites from which Eliot took his inspiration and the title name for each of the poems. To celebrate our tenth wedding anniversary in September 2011, we finally made the journey described below.

"BURNT NORTON" (1935)

In September 1934, Eliot was visiting in Chipping Campden a woman (he was separated from his wife, Vivian) by the name of Emily Hale, with whom he had been on the verge of marrying twenty years before. Instead, he married Vivian Haigh-Wood in 1915. By 1927, Eliot was estranged from Vivian and living separately from her. He had reconnected with Emily, and saw her each summer when she stayed with her aunt and uncle in Chipping Campden. One day Eliot and Emily wandered onto the grounds of the 1,700-acre estate owned (since 1753) by the Earls of Harrowby. The estate takes its name from the original manor house which was called "Norton" before it was burnt to the ground by its owner, Sir William Kyte, who died in the fire. Hence, "Burnt" Norton. The manor house is located about two miles outside of Chipping Campden. Adjacent to the manor house there is a rose garden. Connected to the garden down a long brick alley lie two large concrete pools that are empty and overgrown with moss.

Here is Eliot's description of the rose garden and the dry, concrete pools:

> Footfalls echo in the memory
> Down the passage which we did not take
> Towards the door we never opened
> Into the rose-garden. My words echo
> Thus, in your mind.
> But to what purpose
> Disturbing the dust on a bowl of rose-leaves
> I do not know.
> Other echoes
> Inhabit the garden. Shall we follow?
> Quick, said the bird, find them, find them,

Round the corner. Through the first gate,
Into our first world, shall we follow
The deception of the thrush? Into our first world.
There they were, dignified, invisible,
Moving without pressure, over the dead leaves,
In the autumn heat, through the vibrant air,
And the bird called, in response to
The unheard music hidden in the shrubbery,
And the unseen eyebeam crossed, for the roses
Had the look of flowers that are looked at.
There they were as our guest, accepted and accepting.
So we moved, and they, in a formal pattern,
Along the empty alley, into the box circle,
To look down into the drained pool.
Dry the pool, dry concrete, brown edged,
And the pool was filled with water out of sunlight,
And the lotus rose, quietly, quietly,
The surface glittered out of heart of light,
And they were behind us, reflected in the pool.
Then a cloud passed, and the pool was empty.
Go, said the bird, for the leaves were full of children,
Hidden excitedly, containing laughter.
Go, go, go, said the bird: human kind
Cannot bear very much reality.
Time past and time future
What might have been and what has been
Point to one end, which is always present.[1]

Our visit to Burnt Norton took place on September 4, 2011. Mary Lou and I walked from Chipping Campden to Burnt Norton, just like Tom and Emily—a two-mile walk out into the lovely countryside along the road to Stratford. About one and a quarter miles from town, there is an unmarked turn onto the estate road. Sheep grazed along the road. Every direction you turned was a

---

1. Eliot, *Collected Poems*, 175–76.

perfect Cotswold scene. Continuing the final three-quarters of a mile, we at last came to the manor house. We were greeted by Lady Harrowby (Caroline Sandon), wife of the eighth Earl of Harrowby (Dudley Adrian Conroy Ryder, a/k/a Conroy Sandon). She graciously showed us the grounds, beginning with the rose garden Eliot mentions in the poem. Nevertheless, as Caroline explained, the garden we saw is not exactly the same garden Eliot would have seen. In 1934, the manor house was not occupied (the owners at that time were Conroy's grandparents), but later when the sixth Earl Harrowby did occupy the house, he and his wife completely changed the design of the rose garden.

Going past the rose garden, we walked under a large brick arch and down a long brick pathway for approximately 100 yards to the "box circle" (which does not exist today because the boxwood shrubbery has been replaced and the layout was redesigned in 1934). In front of the box circle are two large concrete pools—one rectangular (intended for swimming, but apparently never used because the sides are too steep) and the other in the shape of a capital "D." Just as Eliot described the pools, they are still "dry" (without water) and "brown" (covered with moss).

Caroline confirmed that Eliot and Emily trespassed onto the estate, since they had not been granted permission to enter. Caroline believes Eliot and Emily entered, not by the road we had taken, but on a pathway, which had several gates, that started just outside Chipping Campden. Local residents in 1934 would have known of the garden and the pools and could have told Emily that it was a must-see sight. Eliot and Emily often took long walks in the countryside around the village.

After showing us the grounds, Caroline said to stay as long as we pleased and that we probably wanted to sit and reread the poem. We gladly accepted the suggestion, and sat in the box circle and read portions of the poem. We left as we came, on foot.

"EAST COKER" (1940)

East Coker is a beautiful, small village on the outskirts of Yeovil (about fifty miles south of Bath). It was the ancestral home of Eliot's family, before Eliot's ancestor, one Andrew Eliot (1627–1703), left East Coker in the seventeenth century to travel to Massachusetts. Andrew never returned to the village but stayed in America and thus began the illustrious American branch of the Eliot family. Eliot visited the village three times (in 1936, 1937, and 1939). According to the small booklet from Eliot's memorial service available for sale at the parish church of St. Michael and All Angels, about a decade before his death in 1965 he left instructions that his ashes were to be buried in the west end of the church.

Eliot's treatment of East Coker in the poem focuses on the village, and does not even mention the church itself. He described the village as follows:

> Now the light falls
> Across the open field, leaving the deep lane
> Shuttered with branches, dark in the afternoon,
> Where you lean against a bank while a van passes,
> And the deep lane insists on the direction
> Into the village, in the electric heat
> Hypnotized. In a warm haze the sultry light
> Is absorbed, not refracted, by grey stone.
> The dahlias sleep in the empty silence.
> Wait for the early owl.[2]

On September 2, 2011, we hired Graham Abotts to drive us from Bath to East Coker. While he had heard of the village, I'm not at all sure he had heard of Eliot or the Quartets. After about a two-hour drive (fifty miles on back roads takes time), we approached the village down a long lane edged by high hedges until we found ourselves in a small village (800 homes according to a guide book, but I did not have a sense that there were that many houses). We knew we were looking for a church, but did not know the name—having the

2. Ibid., 182.

name would have made no difference in our locating the church in this tiny village. Fortunately, we saw a church on a hill, at the highest point in the village, so we headed there.

Indeed, the church was St Michael's—a very old stone building with a Norman tower. Situated on the side of the hill, the church was surrounded on three sides by grave stones which appeared to be quite old (I wonder where contemporary folks are buried). The church door was not locked and we entered to find an interior that is best described as faded, but then again, what you might expect in a very old Anglican church in the English countryside. Inside we found no one in authority. Upon entering we were drawn to the right of the doorway, toward the west wall of the nave. There in the corner is a simple plaque (reading "Of your charity pray for the repose of the soul of Thomas Sterns Eliot, Poet") on the wall above where the ashes of Eliot were buried on Easter Sunday, 1965. That's about all there is. No admission charge at the door. No tour guide available. No tee shirts with "TSE" imprinted or memorabilia for sale. In the track rack there were a few cards for sale and a lone copy of *Four Quartets*. Money was to be deposited in a small wall safe—the honor system in effect.

What a truly fitting memorial to the man who Louis Menand calls "the most important figure in twentieth English language culture."[3] Why? Because this place testifies to the fact that those who cared most for Eliot the man internalized what he had written in "East Coker":

> The only wisdom we can hope to acquire
> Is the wisdom of humility: humility is endless?[4]

Moreover, the larger public who care about Eliot have respected the sanctity of this place and not allowed it to become commercialized.

A caveat must be made—in 2011 there was under consideration by the South Somerset District Council a proposal for significant development of a major housing and employment complex

---

3. Menard, "Practical Cat," para. 3.

4. Eliot, *Collected Poems*, 185.

between Yeovil and East Coker. Critics of the project asserted such development would destroy the pastoral beauty of the countryside around East Coker. Eliot fans from around the world were asked to write to the Council urging that East Coker be preserved in its current state and not enveloped by modern development. Accordingly, on September 21, 2011, I wrote Mr. Ric Pallister, OBE, Leader of the South Somerset District Council as follows: "The village of East Coker remains an important symbol of Eliot's past and, therefore, an especially meaningful place for readers of Eliot's great poetry. Moreover, given the context of its wartime composition and the poem's impact on the emotional health and resolve of the British nation in the 1940s, East Coker is a powerful symbol for future generations that should not be lost. Its role in inspiring future generations will be diminished if the character of this autonomous village (separated from Yeovil by countryside) is lost due to development. Please consider preserving East Coker as it is today, so that visitors from around the world can journey to East Coker to visit the memorial to Eliot in St. Michael's and experience the village immortalized in the poem."

"THE DRY SALVAGES" (1941)

In a note before the poem, Eliot wrote that the Dry Salvages "is a small group of rocks, with a beacon, off the northeast coast of Cape Ann, Massachusetts."[5] This small group of rocks lies about three miles off the shore, but are hidden in part by a large island. Working from a photograph on the website for the Captain's House, a bed and breakfast in Rockport, Massachusetts (69 Marmion Way), we were able to find the location where the internet photograph had been taken, and indeed were able to see the Dry Salvages, barely, off the shore. We inquired inside the Captain's House whether there was a better point from which to observe the rocks. Tim Parker, a transplanted Brit from the south of England, offered the view from his second-story bedroom. We accepted, and were

5. Ibid., 191.

able to get a better view over the intervening island and actually see the complete Dry Salvages to the east of the island.

Although born (1888) and reared in St. Louis, Eliot spent summers with his grandfather who owned a summer house in Gloucester, Massachusetts, a few miles south of Rockport. Eliot learned to sail at an early age, and sailed the waters around Cape Ann many summers, one time sailing all the way to Maine. I surmise that Eliot first encountered the Dry Salvages around 1900, so this location of the Quartets was clearly the first site he visited. Like Eliot, it was our first stop on August 31, 2011 on our journey to the four sites named in the Quartets. We had made one earlier attempt to see the Dry Salvages in 2009 on a driving trip to Maine, but had been unsuccessful. Upon reflection I have decided we looked north from Halibut Point and we should have looked southeast instead. Next time we'll take a boat and really get close to the rocks.

Eliot's brief poetic description of the rocks reads:

> And the ragged rock in the restless waters,
> Waves wash over it, fogs conceal it;
> On a halcyon day it is merely a monument,
> In navigable weather it is always a seamark
> To lay a course by: but in the somber season
> Or the sudden fury, is what it always was.[6]

His poems may often be inscrutable, but in the case of the Quartets, Eliot was on record as saying the poems were about experiencing incarnation ("The hint half guessed, the gift half understood, is / Incarnation").[7] About fifteen lines earlier in the poem before the reference to incarnation, he writes about apprehending the "point of intersection of the timeless / With time."[8] This very graphic visual image is what I have referred to as Eliot's "divine geometry" (see chapter 4). The vertical plane of the timeless element is said to intersect with the horizontal plane of time—the plane on which we find ourselves. That intersection where the planes meet

6. Ibid., 195.
7. Ibid., 199.
8. Ibid., 198.

is where incarnation can be observed and experienced, be it in terms of art, music, literature, or spirituality. Eliot's point is clear—the timeless dimension can be known within the plane of ordinary living. Eliot was most likely introduced to this visual image of intersecting planes in reading Evelyn Underhill's book *Mysticism: A Study in the Nature and Development of Spiritual Consciousness* while he was studying at Harvard (the Harvard Library has his original notes he made on the Underhill book).

This digression about intersecting planes is the predicate for my suggested reading of Eliot's description of "The Dry Salvages" itself, which is quoted above. The rocks and water are a metaphor for incarnation. The rocks form the vertical plane and intersect the horizontal plane of the water. The "restless waters" is a phrase describing human existence itself. In good times ("halcyon day"), incarnation may be forgotten, "it is merely a monument." Other times incarnation lies hidden, we choose to ignore it. When we want to go somewhere it can be a guidepost, a "seamark to lay a course by." Most importantly, in times of trouble ("somber season or sudden fury"), we ignore it at our peril because it is always there ("what it always was") and we may crash into it.

"LITTLE GIDDING" (1942)

Eliot was an Honorary Fellow of Magdalene College, Cambridge, and on May 25, 1936 he was escorted to Little Gidding by the Dean of the College, the Reverend Hugh Fraser Stewart and his wife. Eliot was aware of the history of the religious community established by Nicholas Ferrar (a member of the Virginia Company which established the American colony) in 1636, and no doubt wanted to see what was left of the original community. Ferrar had had a distinguished career in business and government, but chose to withdraw from active life and create a community of men and women who would live a monastic-style life in community. The place surely had a special appeal to Eliot because it was an Anglican religious community and definitely "royalist" in its politics in the seventeenth century (recall Eliot described himself as a "classicist in literature, royalist in politics and an Anglo-Catholic in religion")[9]. King Charles I visited Little Gidding twice—in 1642 and again in retreat after defeat at the battle of Naseby in May 1645 ("at night like a broken king" in the poem). Previously, it had been thought that Oliver Cromwell's forces ransacked the church and the Ferrar manor house, but recent research disputes such action. In any event the little church was renovated in 1714, and a new façade built. The tomb of Ferrar remained in front of the door to the church. The original manor house was destroyed, and in 1848 a new house was built (now known as "Ferrar House," a retreat center) which stands about fifty yards from the church. (There is a quite impressive virtual tour of Little Gidding and a wealth of information at www.littlegiddingchurch.org.uk.)

Although Eliot visited Little Gidding in May, the poem in the scheme of *Four Quartets* is assigned to the position of the "winter poem" in the set. He begins his description with a reference to the hedges being "[w]hite again, in May, with voluptuary sweetness." Obviously, "white again" refers to the hedges being white with snow in the winter and in May with flowers. Of all the Quartets, the description of the church at Little Gidding is the most extended:

> If you came this way,
> Taking the route you would be likely to take
> From the place you would be likely to come from,
> If you came this way in may time, you would find the hedges
> White again, in May, with voluptuary sweetness.
> It would be the same at the end of the journey,
> If you came at night like a broken king,
> If you came by day not knowing what you came for,
> It would be the same, when you leave the rough road
> And turn behind the pig-sty to the dull façade
> And the tombstone. And what you thought you came for
> Is only a shell, a husk of meaning
> From which the purpose breaks only when it is fulfilled
> If at all. Either you had no purpose

9. Eliot, *For Lancelot Andrewes*, 7.

Or the purpose is beyond the end you figured
And is altered in fulfillment. There are other places
Which also are the world's end, some at the sea jaws,
Or over a dark lake, in a desert or a city—
But this is the nearest in place and time,
Now and in England.[10]

On September 5, 2011, we were driven by a full-time farmer, part-time commercial driver, Robin Dale, from Chipping Campden to Little Gidding, which is located off the A1 between Peterborough and Huntingdon. We approached from the south through the village of Great Gidding to a road with a sign for "Little Gidding." The road was more of a driveway that ran about 200 yards to a hamlet and car park. (Leaving Little Gidding, we passed by the third "Gidding" in the area, Steeple Gidding.) St. John's Church, Little Gidding, Cambridgeshire, was approximately fifty yards away. St. John's remains a working church, albeit infrequently judging by the list of services posted on the bulletin board on the walkway leading to the church. The priest-in-charge is a woman.

The rectangular tomb of Nicholas Ferrar is still situated immediately in front of the "dull façade" (Eliot's words). Just like St. Michael's, no one in authority was present, and the door was unlocked, so we entered. The interior was very bright due to the stained glass portions of the windows being surrounded by clear glass so sunlight shone through. A beautiful brass chandelier hung above the congregational seating which was in the monastic style of rows on each side of the church facing each other with a center aisle decorated in a checkerboard mosaic pattern. There was a very simple altar in the east end of the nave. Thankfully, there was absolutely no commercialization of any kind in St. John's. A few note cards and pictures were for sale in the track rack; once again, it was the honor system as far as payment was concerned—you stuffed the money in a small slot in the wall safe.

---

10. Eliot, *Collected Poems*, 201–02.

While the physical description of Little Gidding was quoted above, the better description of what the place "feels" like follows immediately after in the poem where Eliot writes:

> You are not here to verify,
> Instruct yourself, or inform curiosity
> Or carry report. You are here to kneel
> Where prayer has been valid.[11]

This is truly a place, "[w]here prayer has been valid." (In Ferrar's day someone in the community was in the church praying and reading the Bible twenty-four hours a day, each day of the year.)

Eliot concedes "[t]here are other places / which also are the world's end,"[12] which is that intersection line between the plane of time (our world) and the plane of the timeless dimension. Nevertheless, Little Gidding "is the nearest, in place and time, / Now and in England."[13] Indeed, remember this poem was written in 1942 at the height of World War II—Eliot needed to find an intersection in England not only for artistic reasons but to inspire hope in his readers that life would go on notwithstanding the horrors that were being experienced in England. He concludes Section I emphatically:

> Here, the intersection of the timeless moment
> Is England and nowhere. Never and always.[14]

It seems to me that Eliot's overarching theme in *Four Quartets* is the Divine (incarnation) in art, music, literature, and spirituality can be experienced in our everyday existence. Yes, there are places where it is easier for one reason or another for us to apprehend the intersection between the planes. Little Gidding, to me, is one of those places. Nevertheless, the intersection is always there; we just need to be looking.

We looked for Eliot's church in London—St. Stephen's on the Gloucester Road north of Cromwell Road in South Kensington.

11. Ibid., 201.
12. Ibid., 201.
13. Ibid., 201.
14. Ibid., 201.

Unfortunately, the church was locked and we were unable to see inside. (There is a photograph of the beautiful interior on the cover of a book published in 2010 by Barry Spurr entitled, *Anglo-Catholic in Religion/T.S. Eliot and Christianity*.) Eliot worshipped at St. Stephen's for over thirty years and served as a church warden for many of those years.

Chapter 4

Divine Geometry

What I have termed "divine geometry" provides two visual images to assist the reader with understanding the central themes of *Four Quartets*. In the opening section of "Burnt Norton," Eliot alerts the reader to something that the four poems are about, without specifically naming what that is—

> What might have been and what has been
> Point to one end, which is always present.[1]

It is not until the last section of "The Dry Salvages" that the "one end, which is always present" is finally revealed as incarnation—

> The hint half guessed, the gift half understood, is Incarnation.[2]

Note the absence of the capitalized article "the" in front of the word "Incarnation." The Incarnation is most often associated in the Christian understanding of the term with the Divine becoming a man in the person of Jesus Christ and being in the world. Nevertheless, the absence of the preceding article is surely intentional on Eliot's part, intended to have a meaning. I read the absence of the article as Eliot's way of alerting the reader to a much broader

---

1. Eliot, *Collected Poems*, 176.
2. Ibid., 199.

reading of incarnation to include transcendence in other fields, such as art, music, literature, as well as, of course, spirituality.

In the last section of "Burnt Norton" for example, the poem speaks of words and music reaching into "stillness." A Chinese jar "still moves perpetually in its stillness." As discussed below "stillness" equates to the place where the Divine is encountered. In his book, *T. S. Eliot and the Essay*, Professor G. Douglas Atkins defines incarnation expansively to mean "truth embodied." Thus, words, music, and a Chinese jar can reach into stillness and embody truth—that is, to participate on some level with divinity.

Without a specific reference to incarnation, Eliot in section V of "The Dry Salvages" writes about "the point of intersection of the timeless / With time."[3] In section I of "Little Gidding" there is "the intersection of the timeless moment / Is England and no where / Never and always."[4] In the London Blitz scene in "Little Gidding" the "compound ghost" and poet walk the devastated streets "at this intersection time." So, what does intersection have to do with incarnation? The answer is everything.

Incarnation is that loci of points where the Divine breaks into the life of man. In trying to explain this point to classes I have taught about *Four Quartets*, I have used the visual image of intersecting planes to show that incarnation can be thought of as the intersection of the plane of time (our human time) with the timeless plane of the Divine. In figure 1 there is a schematic showing the intersecting planes with Incarnation represented as the dotted line where the planes meet.

3. Eliot, *Collected Poems*, 198.
4. Ibid., 201.

Figure 1

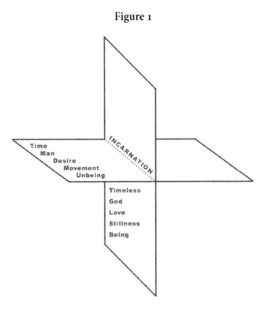

Without an understanding of incarnation, however, a different visual representation is shown in figure 2 below.

Figure 2

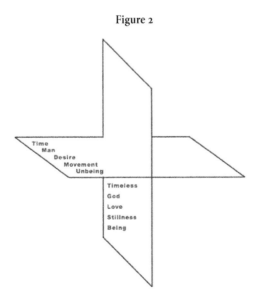

The two planes exist ("one end, which is always present"), but we may not see the possibility that the Divine has entered our world, and indeed can be experienced in our lifetime. Eliot's point, I believe, is precisely depicted in figure 1 because of incarnation ("truth embodied") we can experience the Divine in art, music, literature, and spirituality. It could be said that *Four Quartets* is about the experience of finding the line of intersection between the planes of time and timeless.

While it is not known for sure what source inspired Eliot's motif of intersecting planes, there is some evidence of a possible source. While studying at Harvard in 1911 Eliot read Evelyn Underhill's classic study of mysticism (*Mysticism: A Study in the Nature and Development of Man's Spiritual Consciousness*) and attended her class on this subject. Evelyn Underhill (1875–1941) was probably the most influential scholar writing about mysticism in the twentieth century. Lyndall Gordon, in her biography of Eliot (*T. S. Eliot/An Imperfect Life*), wrote that Eliot made copious notes from the Underhill book. Within Underhill's book there are numerous uses of a variety of planes—"two planes of existence," "two planes of nature," "spiritual plane" versus the "material plane," and "transcendent" versus the "phenomenal plane." It seems likely that as early as 1911 Eliot was introduced to the visual image of intersecting planes.

Underhill was not the only early twentieth-century author who saw the intersection of the planes of man and the Divine. Karl Barth made a much more explicit statement in his *Epistle to the Romans* (1915):

> In this name two worlds meet and go apart, two planes intersect, the one known and the other unknown. The known plane is God's creation, fallen out of its union with Him and therefore the world of the 'flesh' needing redemption, the world of men, and of time, and of things—our world. This known plane is intersected by another plane that is unknown—the world of the Father, of the Primal Creation, and of the final Redemption. The relation between us and God, between this world and His world, presses for recognition, but the line of intersection

is not self-evident. The point on the line of intersection at which the relation becomes observable and observed is Jesus, Jesus of Nazareth, the historical Jesus.[5]

I have been unable to find any evidence that Eliot read *Epistle to the Romans*, but in 1915 it was a significant theological work, and given Eliot's interest in philosophy and religion, Eliot may have read it.

There is a second visual image which may be useful in helping a reader understand Eliot's repeated usage of the terms "still point," "stillness," and "be still" in the poems.

In figure 3 there is a schematic of the still point.

Figure 3

The still point—It does not move

At the very center of an axle of a wheel, there is a point which does not move while the rest of the axle, spokes of the wheel, and rim move about that fixed center point. The still point is an alternate

5. Barth, *The Epistle to the Romans*, 29.

way of envisioning incarnation where divine transcendence can be experienced, especially by saints, who then mediate their experience of the Divine to the rest of the world who exist on the rim of the wheel. Historically, it may have been saints who mediated the Divine to mankind, but today it is poets like Eliot who describe the experience of Divine transcendence to the world at large.

There is Biblical foundation for stillness as a means to know the Divine. Psalm 62, for instance, says: "For God alone I wait silently; my deliverance comes from him." Psalm 46 reads: "Be still and know that I am God." And the prophet Isaiah (30:15) found strength in stillness: "In stillness and quiet there lie my strength." (A more modern translation reads "In calm detachment lies your safety, your strength in quiet trust.")

Chapter 5

Mysticism

Intelligence pushed to its depth leads to mysticism.

T. S. ELIOT

To many the idea of mysticism is probably not part of their experience. We may have no clue as to what the term even means. On the other hand, our view may be that it has something to do with magic or the occult. Evelyn Underhill provides a short definition: "Of all those forms of life and thought with which humanity has fed its craving for truth, mysticism alone postulates . . . not only the existence of the Absolute, but also this link: the possibility first of knowing, finally of attaining it."[1] Underhill's description seems to rhyme with the idea depicted in chapter 4 insofar as man on the plane of time has the potential of knowing the transcendental plane of the Divine (due to incarnation). This chapter will explore what mysticism is and why *Four Quartets* is a mystical writing. Finally, the chapter will address why anyone might wish to read the Quartets as an introduction to mysticism.

1. Underhill, *Mysticism*, 23.

In her book, Underhill takes almost 500 pages to fully explicate the parameters of mysticism, but she summarizes what it is in this longer definition than the one quoted above:

> Mysticism, then is not an opinion: it is not a philosophy. It has nothing in common with the pursuit of occult knowledge. On the one hand it is not merely the power of contemplating Eternity: on the other, it is not to be identified with any kind of religious queerness. It is the name of that organic process which involves the perfect consummation of the Love of God: the achievement here and now of the immortal heritage of man. Or, if you like this better—for this means exactly the same thing—it is the art of establishing his conscious relation with the Absolute.[2]

Underhill then proposes "four other rules or notes" as tests to be applied to any specific claim of mystical experience: (1) "True mysticism is active and practical, not passive and theoretical," (2) "its aims are wholly transcendental and spiritual," (3) the divine is the sole object of the mystic's love, and (4) living union with the divine is attained by an arduous psychological and spiritual process which she calls the "Mystic Way."[3]

Point 1 is that mysticism is based on experience, not theory. It is not obtained by reading and study, although those activities will surely accompany the mystic's journey. It is an act of love involving surrender of the self to the Divine. Point 2 is that the mystic is not seeking supernatural powers for the increase of power, virtue, happiness, or knowledge. "He possesses God, and needs nothing more."[4] Point 3 is key—the driving force is love, not knowledge. "Mystic Love is a total dedication of the will; the deep-seated desire and tendency of the soul towards its Source."[5] The heart, not reason, leads the mystic to the Divine. Finally, point 4 is "it shows itself not merely as an attitude of the mind and heart but as a form

---

2. Ibid., 81.
3. Ibid., 81.
4. Ibid., 84.
5. Ibid., 85.

of organic life."[6] It is not merely a theory of the intellect or a hunger, but the organizing of the whole self due to that hunger. One's entire character is re-organized in the interest of the transcendental life. Spiritual desires are seen to be useless unless they cause the self to move to the divine reality.

Once more, let me quote Underhill as she sums up mysticism. To sum up, mysticism is seen to be a highly specialized form of that:

> search for reality, for heightened and completed life, which we have found to be a constant characteristic of human consciousness. It is largely prosecuted by that "spiritual spark," that transcendental faculty which, though the life of our life, remains below the threshold in ordinary men. Emerging from its hiddenness in the mystic, it gradually becomes the dominant factor in his life; subduing to its service, and enhancing by saving contact with reality, those vital powers of love and will which we attribute to the heart, rather than those of mere reason and perception, which we attribute to the head. Under the spur of this love and will, the whole personality rises in the acts of contemplation and ecstasy to a level of consciousness at which it becomes aware of a new field of perception. By this awareness, by this "loving sight," it is stimulated to a new life in accordance with the Reality which it has beheld. So strange and exalted is this life, that it never fails to provoke either the anger or the admiration of other men.[7]

With a better understanding of mysticism let us turn to the question of why *Four Quartets* can be considered a mystical writing. Beginning as early as 1911 when he was a graduate student at Harvard, and perhaps earlier, Eliot showed an interest in the subject of mysticism. We know he read the Underhill book in 1911 because he made notes of his reading (the notes are in the archives of Harvard). He wrote about the subject of mysticism on several occasions and offered his own definitions: (1) "Intelligence pushed to its depth

6. Ibid., 90.
7. Ibid., 93–94.

leads to mysticism,"[8] and (2) "All human faculties pushed to their depths ends in mysticism."[9] Eliot quotes or alludes to numerous mystical writings in the Quartets—John of the Cross, Dame Julian of Norwich, *The Cloud of Unknowing*, and *The Bhagavad Gita*, to name the principal sources. Finally, the poems can be read to follow the so-called "Mystic Way" which Underhill found to be the psychological and spiritual process by which a mystic arrives at union with the Divine.

Underhill identifies five stages on the journey to the Divine:

1. Awaking—the self becomes joyfully conscious of divine reality. I choose to call this experience the "Aha" and it is described in the first section of "Burnt Norton" in the scene in the rose garden.

2. Purgation—a painful stage where the self tries to eliminate by discipline and mortification all of the earthly things that separate the self from the Divine. "East Coker" (section III) quotes at length John of the Cross regarding those things which must be given up.

3. Dark Night of the Soul (or "mystic death") where in spite of the "Aha" and experiencing the presence of the Divine, the soul instead experiences an intense sense of the absence of the Divine. Here the "I" must be overcome, and therefore this stage is sometimes called "spiritual crucifixion." As Eliot describes the Dark Night in "East Coker" the soul must "wait without hope;" that is, must be passive.

4. Illumination—this stage typically follows Purgation and the Dark Night, and is much like a second or enhanced "Aha". The apprehension of the Divine is greater, but still not in union with the Divine. Compared to the second and third stages it is a state of happiness. In terms of the Divine Geometry, it is the recognition or perception of the intersection of the two planes—the Divine is truly present in the plane of time and man. The vertical or transcendental plane can be

8. Lobb, *Words in Time*, 107.
9. Ibid., 107.

seen. "The Dry Salvages" (section V) describes illumination in terms of apprehending "[t]he point of intersection of the timeless with time, an occupation for the saint."[10]

5. Union—this is the goal of the mystic journey. The Divine is not only perceived and experienced but the self and the Divine are one. Some mystics call this state a "Mystical Marriage" between the soul and the Divine. This stage is not easily identified in the poems, but surely must have something to do with the joyful conclusion of the final poem, "Little Gidding":

> And all shall be well and
> All manner of thing shall be well
> When the tongues of flame are in-folded
> Into the crowned knot of fire
> And the fire and the rose are one.[11]

Before proceeding with a more in-depth tracing of the Mystic Way in the poems, it is important to have an understanding of the common structure of the four poems. The poems themselves will be referred to using the following notation: BN—"Burnt Norton," EC—"East Coker," DS—"The Dry Salvages," and LG—"Little Gidding". Each poem has five sections or movements (in keeping with the musical theme of quartets). The sections will be referred to with Roman numerals. Each section has two subsections which shall be referred to as "a" or "b." The "a" subsections of each section tend to have a more temporal viewpoint (that is, our time or horizontal plane) compared to the "b" subsections which tend to have a more timeless or eternal perspective. The corresponding sections likewise tend to have a similar point of view. Section I posits the moment in which the Divine is experienced. Section II will often deny to some extent the experience dealt with in section I.

Section III suggests a turning point, characterized by acceptance, reconciliation, and transformation. Section IV—always the shortest in length—describes in lyrical terms some communion

10. Eliot, *Collected Poems*, 198.

11. Ibid., 209.

35

between the Divine and the temporal. Finally, except for DS, section V has a meditation on language and writing and closes with a recapitulation of themes in earlier sections of the particular poem.

With the structure of the poems in mind, let us look at how the Mystic Way finds its way through the poems. As mentioned above, the "Aha" takes place in the rose garden in "Burnt Norton" (Ib), and is a sudden realization of a reality that is outside the plane of time. There were unseen children referred to as "our guests" whose presence was nevertheless felt. A bird called in response to "unheard music." An "unseen eyebeam" seemed to look at the roses in the garden. The poet and the children move in tandem down an alley to look at an empty pool. Amazingly, the empty, dry pool was "filled with water out of sunlight" and reflections of the unseen children were momentarily seen by the poet. The experience is short-lived, however, because a cloud passes and there is no longer any sunlight to fill the pool. The bird says "go" because "human kind cannot bear very much reality." BN concludes at the end of section V with the thought that encounter with the Divine is always available, but that there is wasted time before and after the encounter. Clearly, the "Aha" awakens us to the presence of the Divine and whets the appetite to future encounters along the Mystic Way.

The "Aha" sets the soul on a journey, a quest. The next step on that journey is known as the "Purgative Way." Both the Purgative Way and the third stage, The Dark Night, were subjects of writings by the contemplative theologian and poet, John of the Cross (1512–1591). As we'll see below, Eliot drew heavily from the text of *The Ascent of Mount Carmel/The Dark Night*. There are four parts to this work: the sketch of Mount Carmel, a poem of eight stanzas, and a two-part commentary and treatise. The drawing or sketch is a one-page summary of John's teaching. Eliot quoted selections from the sketch in BN and EC. The poem too is a summary of the teaching and is further explained in the two treatises.

It is somewhat confusing because John calls the journey itself to the Divine "The Dark Night," but then in his second treatise entitled "The Dark Night" instead deals with what he calls "passive purgation," but which I have instead chosen to call "The Dark

Night." Purgation or "active purgation" (in John's terms) is the elimination of those elements of normal experience which are obstacles to harmony with the Divine.

In EC (IIIb) Eliot makes reference to the "Aha" Experience ("echoed ecstasy not lost . . . ") and says that in order to arrive there "you must go by a way wherein there is no ecstasy."[12] This is the Purgative Way and is described in EC by paraphrase and lifing language from John's sketch of how to attain the summit of Mount Carmel:

> Shall I say it again? In order to arrive there,
> To arrive where you are, to get from where you are not,
> You must go by a way wherein there is no ecstasy.
> In order to arrive at what you do not know
> You must go by a way which is the way of ignorance.
> In order to possess what you do not possess
> You must go by the way of dispossession.
> In order to arrive at what you are not
> You must go through the way in which you are not.
> And what you do not know is the only thing you know
> And what you own is what you do not own
> And where you are is where you are not.[13]

John of the Cross in his drawing puts it this way:

> To come to the pleasure you have not
> you must go by a way in which you enjoy not
> To come to the knowledge you have not
> you must go by a way in which you know not
> To come to the possession you have not
> you must go by a way in which you possess not
> To come to be what you are not
> you must go by a way in which you are not[14]

---

12. Ibid., 187.

13. Ibid., 187.

14. John of the Cross, *Collected Works*, 67.

As you can see, what is called for is "active" purgation in that one must take steps to embrace ignorance, dispossession of things, and loss of ego.

In contrast the Dark Night is "passive;" the spiritual pilgrim is called upon to do essentially nothing but wait (Underhill says that "impotence, blankness, solitude" describe this stage). More troubling is the experience of the utter loss or absence of the Divine. This stage is seen by mystics as the final purification of the will, or in other words, the self learns to cease to be its own center. Underhill describes this stage as follows: "Only when [the mystic] learns to cease thinking of himself at all . . . when he abolishes even such selfhood as lies in a desire for the sensible presence of God, will that harmony [with the Divine] be attained."[15] Eliot in EC (IIIa) describes the Dark Night as follows:

> I said to my soul, be still, and wait without hope
> For hope would be hope for the wrong thing; wait without love
> For love would be love of the wrong thing; there is yet faith
> For the faith and the love and the hope are all in the waiting.
> Wait without thought, for you are not ready for thought:
> So the darkness shall be the light, and the stillness the dancing.[16]

As stated in this quotation, out of darkness comes light and dancing. Earlier in BN the idea of "dance" being present at the still point was introduced and "there is only the dance." Dance is closely related to the word "pattern" (a word used ten times in the four poems). In the final section of LG it is written that a "pattern of timeless moments" is nothing less than "history" itself. In other words the Divine is continually present in the temporal plane, but we will not know that unless we are able to decode the pattern, the dance.

Following the "Aha" (awaking) and purification (both active and passive), the self finds it is able to apprehend another order of reality; in other words, sees the possibility of the vertical plane of transcendence. The apprehension does not create the vertical plane; it has always been there even if not previously seen (all time

15. Underhill, *Mysticism*, 399.

16. Eliot, *Collected Poems*, 186.

points to one end "which is always present"—BN(Ib)). The pre-
liminaries are over and there is a new and solid certitude about the
Divine—an enlightenment, an illumination. Nevertheless, because
the "I" still exists, the fifth and final stage of union has still not
been attained. Lest we assume illumination is limited to the spiritual, Underhill reminds:

> Many a great painter, philosopher, or poet, perhaps every
> inspired musician, has known this indescribable inebria-
> tion of Reality in those moments of transcendence in
> which the masterpieces were conceived. This is the 'sav-
> ing madness' of which Plato speaks in the 'Phaedrus,'
> the ecstasy of the 'God-intoxicated man,' the lover, the
> prophet, and the poet 'drunk with life.'[17]

In DS(Vb) the point of Four Quartets is revealed—"[t]he hint
half guessed, the gift half understood, is Incarnation."[18] Eliot has said
that his intention with the Quartets was to write about the experience of believing a dogma of the Church, in this case specifically the
dogma of the Incarnation. Apprehension of "the point of intersection of the timeless [the vertical plane of transcendence] with time"[19]
seems the essence of the stage of illumination insofar as another
order of reality is perceived. Notice that illumination is something
that is "given" as a result of "death in love" [Dark Night], rejection of
the self and self-surrender [purgation]. It is "an occupation for the
saint." "For most of us" illumination will not be experienced, and
we'll be limited to the occasional "Aha" experience.

The four initial stages of the Mystic Way seem to be experienced on the horizontal plane of human experience. With the
fifth and final stage (Union), the action moves to the vertical plane,
which represents a different dimension of time (eternity). (A comparison should be made with the point of view of Ravi Ravindra
in his book, *The Pilgrim Soul*, in which he asserts that eternity is
not an extension or a continuation of time, but instead refers to
a dimension of being) The opening of Little Gidding tips us off

17. Underhill, *Mysticism*, 235.
18. Eliot, *Collected Poems*, 199.
19. Ibid., 198.

that a different dimension of time will be dealt with in the last quartet. "Midwinter spring is its own season" which is said to be "sempiternal" (eternal). Moreover, "this is the spring time/ But not in time's covenant" (that is, the timeless or eternal). In LG(II) this is referred to as "intersection time."

There are additional references to intersection time in LG. First, there is Little Gidding itself, the existing chapel as well as the seventeenth-century community which prayed twenty-four hours a day in the chapel. The stone over the west door of the chapel entrance is still inscribed: "This is none other but the house of God and the gate of heaven." Second, there are "other places / which also are the world's end."[20] The world's end can refer to the very edge of the plane of time where it intersects the transcendent plane. In particular the specific places enumerated in the poem can be associated with other religious sites which, like Little Gidding, are places where the intersection of the planes is most visable, namely, "at the sea jaws," "over a dark lake," "in a city," and "a city." (See chapter 10). Finally, in LG (II) the poet meets a compound ghost following a German bombing raid during the World War II Blitz in London. This scene, which is an homage to Dante's *Inferno*, is described in the poem as taking place in "intersection time." All of these signs point to an exceptional environment for an encounter with the Divine.

What can be said concerning union with the Divine? Actually, very little unless you are one of the few mystics who have been graced with the fifth stage of the Mystic Way. The textbook explanation fails to convey a real understanding: man's will is united with God's will. But what does that mean? Since Union belongs to the vertical plane of being, the supernatural plane, the answer can really only come from the testimony of those persons who have been identified over the years as mystics. That testimony generally has two components: (1) What the mystics say about their transcendental experience, and (2) How their lives were in fact lived due to their transformation. Underhill in her book cites numerous examples of what mystics who reached the fifth stage say about their experience and how their lives were transformed.

20. Ibid., 201.

John of the Cross is a good example of what Union looks like. He explains that the phrase "union of the soul with God" takes place in the intellect, the will and the memory. Its essence is a "likeness of love:"

> The supernatural union exists when God's will and the soul's are in conformity, so that nothing in the one is repugnant to the other. When the soul completely rids itself of what is repugnant and unconformed to the divine will, it rests transformed in God through love.[21]

To a much greater extent than the first four stages described in the Quartets, the fifth stage of Union is dealt with in oblique fashion. At best there are hints and guesses. There is, however, a confidence alluded to that suggests "all shall be well and / All manner of thing shall be well."[22] There are two other quotations from Dame Julian in LG: (1) "Sin is Behovely [necessary], but / All manner of thing shall be well,"[23] and (2) "And all shall be well and / All manner of thing shall be well / By the purification of the motive / In the ground of our beseeching [contemplation]."[24] In LG (IV) George Herbert is echoed in that love is said to be the force that discharges "sin and error," and thus creates the condition for "all shall be well." There is an additional quotation from *The Cloud of Unknowing* which emphasizes the love of the Divine as the catalyst for union: "What weary wretched heart sleeping in sloth, is that, the which is not wakened with the drawing of this love and the voice of this Calling."[25] Eliot chose to quote a portion of this passage (beginning at "with the drawing") in LG (V). The Cloud's quotation mirrors the description of John of the Cross that union is a likeness of love between mystic and Divine.

LG (V) concludes with lines that suggest union of some kind:

A condition of complete simplicity

(costing not less than everything)

---

21. John of the Cross, *Collected Works*, 116.

22. Eliot, *Collected Poems*, 206.

23. Ibid., 205–06.

24. Ibid., 206–07.

25. Ricks and McCue, *The Poems of T. S. Eliot, Vol. 1*, 1042.

> All shall be well and
> All manner of things shall be well
> When the tongues of flame are in-folded
> Into the crowned knot of fire
> And the fire and the rose are one.[26]

There has been much speculation over the years as to the meaning of the fire and the rose being one. Eliot was silent as to his intention with these words. Nevertheless, there is a union of fire and rose which gives rise to a state of wellness, which seems to be the anticipated consequence of man's union with the Divine.

Before addressing why we might want to learn more about mysticism, it is important to know there are two principal traditions of the mystical experience and each is very different from the other in approach: kataphatic (from *kataphasis*, meaning knowledge) and apophatic (from *apophasis* meaing denial; this is also known as the "Via Negativa"). Because of Eliot's reliance on writings by John of the Cross and *The Cloud of Unknowing*, the Quartets present an apophatic approach. The key difference between the two traditions is how the question of "what can be known about God" is answered. Kataphatic mysticism posits that through reason, memory, imagination, will, and ordinary awareness, we can learn what God is like; indeed we can describe God's attributes. This approach assumes that man can acquire knowledge of God. In opposition, the apophatic tradition denies that man on his own can ever know anything about God. Instead, the knowledge of God is a matter of grace, a divine gift. Man is to use intuition, silence, and spiritual awareness to prepare himself, but then must wait for God to reveal himself to man. Thomas Merton sums up the apophatic approach as follows:

> Now, while the Christian contemplative must certainly develop by study, the theological understanding of concepts about God, he is called mainly to penetrate the wordless darkness and apophatic light of an experience beyond concepts, and here he gradually becomes familiar

26. Eliot, *Collected Poems*, 209.

with a God who is "absent" and as it were non-existent to all human experience.[27]

In concluding consideration of mysticism it seems appropriate to ask: "Why should anyone care about the Mystic Way?" Is it merely an historical anomaly which has little relevance in the twenty-first century? What relevance has mysticism for the ordinary, non-mystical person? Once again, Underhill supplies the answer:

> I do not care whether the consciousness be that of artist or musician, striving to catch and fix some aspect of the heavenly light or music, and denying all other aspects of the world in order to devote themselves to this: or of the humble servant of Science purging his intellect that he may look upon her secrets with innocence of eye: whether the higher reality be perceived in the terms of religion, beauty, suffering; of human love, of goodness, or of truth. However widely these forms of transcendence may seem to differ, the mystic experience is the key to them all.[28]

The mystics have led the way; they have shown us the process, the way to transcendence in any field. "To be a mystic is simply to participate here and now in that real and eternal life; in the fullest, deepest sense which is possible to man."[29]

A simple graphic may suffice to summarize why mysticism is important. Recall in chapter 4, figure 3, we saw the spokes of the wheel representing the saints (the mystics) who experience transcendence at the still point and then mediate their experience to everyone else living on the outer rim of the wheel. By participating in the Mystic Way—to whatever degree—we too can touch the vertical plane of truth, beauty, the good—transcendence. Mystics supply the roadmap for a journey to the Divine.

---

27. Shannon, *Thomas Merton's Dark Path*, 11.

28. Underhill, *Mysticism*, 446.

29. Ibid., 447.

Chapter 6

Krishna

Section III of "The Dry Salvages" begins with a most startling statement—"I sometimes wonder if that is what Krishna meant."[1] The other bookend for section III occurs at line 43 where we read: "So Krishna, as when he admonished Arjuna / On the field of battle." Thus, it seems safe to conclude that Section III must have something to do with Krishna and Arjuna, the central figures in *The Bhagavad Gita*. Were it not for this opening line in section III it is most likely I would never have read *The Bhagavad Gita* wherein Krishna plays the central role. So, another reason to read *Four Quartets* is it may lead you to read the Gita.

First, what is the Gita (also known as "the Song of the Lord")? It is a classic of Hindu spirituality written about 150 BCE and forms part of the great Indian war epic, the *Mahabharata*. Similar to the context in which the Quartets were written, the Gita is a wartime story about finding the Divine. The principal characters in the story are Arjuna, a warrior, and his chariot driver, Krishna, who is unknown to Arjuna in the beginning of the story, but who later reveals himself to be a divine power who periodically visits mankind to help restore order especially in times of chaos. There is a civil war between kinsmen in process. The story opens with two armies facing each other and about to engage in battle. Arjuna

---

1. Eliot, *Collected Poems*, 195.

instructs his charioteer, Krishna, to drive part way toward his enemies and halt the chariot. Seeing his kinsmen about to attack, Arjuna refuses to fight. In the ensuing dialogue between Arjuna and Krishna, the latter tries to persuade Arjuna to do his duty as a warrior and fight by arguing two points. First, Arjuna is reminded he is a great warrior and his role and station in life is to fight; indeed, it is his sacred duty to fight. By performing his sacred duty as a warrior, Arjuna will fulfill the will of Krishna and will suffer no ill consequences of his action. Second, in order to do Krishna's will it is necessary for Arjuna to act without worrying about the "fruits of action." In other words, Arjuna should act with detachment which can be achieved in meditation—where one withdraws from both the world and time itself.

Taken at face value, this is a grisly story—kill your relatives and don't give it a second thought. This is most likely not intended as a realistic story at all, but instead is meant to represent a struggle within the mind of Arjuna because he is presented with a conflict situation where the right course of action is not clear. Both choices are bad—fight or flee.

Let's examine the Gita more closely to try to find a reason Eliot would include references to a Hindu text in a poem that otherwise focuses on Western spirituality. Like *Four Quartets*, the Gita describes a journey to the Divine. We learn in the concluding chapter of the Gita that by performing work (action) selflessly without attachment to the outcome ("fruits of action"), and doing this as an act of devotion to Krishna, then one attains spiritual perfection (that is, union with the Divine). Krishna says:

Through devotion he discerns me,
just who and how vast I really am;
and knowing me in reality,
he enters into my presence.

Always performing all actions,
taking refuge in me,

he attains through my grace
the eternal place beyond change.[2]

By inserting in the Quartets an alternate path to the Divine, Eliot seems to make the case that there are indeed alternate paths to the Divine. Unlike orthodox Christianity which asserts an exclusive path to God (through belief in Jesus Christ), "The Dry Salvages" embraces the idea that both Western and Eastern spirituality can lead to the Divine.

Eliot, while a graduate student at Harvard (1911–1912), studied Sanskrit, and the Gita was assigned reading for his course. Eliot read the Gita in its original language. In his 1929 essay on Dante, Eliot called the Gita "the next greatest philosophical poem to *The Divine Comedy* in my experience."[3] Moreover, he expressed some interest in reconciliation of Eastern religious thought and Christianity ("I do think that some of my poetry is peculiar in a kind of poetic fusion of Eastern and Western currents of feeling.")[4]

In order to achieve action with detachment, Krishna strongly recommends that meditation should be practiced. In the sixth book of the Gita, Krishna instructs Arjuna how to meditate:

A man of discipline should always
discipline himself, remain in seclusion
isolated, his thought and self well controlled,
without possession or hope.

He should fix for himself
a firm seat in a pure place,
neither too high nor too low,
covered in cloth, deerskin, or grass.

He should focus his mind and restrain
the activity of his thought and senses;

---

2. *The Bhagavad Gita*, 143.
3. Eliot, *Selected Essays*, 258.
4. Ricks and McCue, *The Poems of T. S. Eliot*, 977.

sitting on that seat, he should practice
discipline for the purification of the self.

He should keep his body, head,
and neck aligned, immobile, steady;
he should gaze at the tip of his nose
and not let his glance wander.

The self tranquil, his fear dispelled,
firm in his vow of celibacy, his mind restrained,
let him sit with discipline,
his thought fixed on me, intent on me.[5]

The importance of meditation as a part of the spiritual journey is addressed in section III of "The Dry Salvages" in the metaphor of the journeys by train and ocean liner:

When the train starts, and the passengers are settled
To fruit, periodicals and business letters
Their faces relax from grief into relief
To the sleepy rhythm of a hundred hours.[6]

During meditation ("At the moment which is not of action or inaction") "time is withdrawn" so that future and past can be considered "with an equal mind."

While meditating on Krishna is important throughout life, it is especially important at death because whatever is on one's mind at death, that is what he'll become in the next life according to Hindu belief. In the eighth book of the Gita, Krishna says:

Whatever being he remembers
when he abandons the body at death,
he enters, Arjuna,
always existing in that being.

5. *The Bhagavad Gita*, 66–67.

6. Eliot, *Collected Poems*, 196.

> Therefore, at all times remember me
> and fight;
> mind and understanding fixed on me,
> free from doubt, you will come to me.[7]

Eliot, on the other hand, recasts these lines as follows: "on whatever sphere of being / The mind of man may be intent / At the time of death—that is the one action / . . . / Which shall fructify in the lives of others."[8] Instead of concentrating on Krishna in order to merge into divinity, Eliot suggests concentrating on the "one action / . . . / Which shall fructify in the lives of others."[9] Although the climax of all four poems is yet to come in section V of "The Dry Salvages," in this context it seems safe to say that it is incarnation which shall "fructify in the lives of others." Since death is a possibility at any moment ("And the time of death is every moment")[10], we should think of incarnation at all times in order to be a significant force for others.

To emphasize the role of action Eliot chose the example of "fisherman sailing / Into the wind's tail," "forever bailing / Setting and hauling," who "suffer the trial and judgment of the sea," but perform their duty (their "real destination"). Seamen as well as everyone else are urged to "fare forward, voyagers." At the same time "do not think of the fruit of action." As the Gita says:

> Be intent on action,
> not on the fruits of action;
> avoid attraction to the fruits
> and attachment to inaction![11]

Finally, the Gita offers advice that applies to anyone on the mystical journey. There is the issue of one's own vocation for the spiritual journey. In book eighteen of the Gita it says: "Better to do

7. *The Bhagavad Gita*, 80.
8. Eliot, *Collected Poems*, 197.
9. Ibid., 197.
10. Ibid., 197.
11. *The Bhagavad Gita*, 38.

one's own duty imperfectly than to do another man's well; during action intrinsic to his being a man avoids guilt."[12] The point is that not everyone is called to completing the journey to union with the divine. In the words of the Gita, it is a matter of God's grace:

> To grace you, Arjuna
> I revealed
> through self-disciplne
> my higher form,
> which no one but you
> has ever beheld.[13]

Eliot did not claim to be a mystic. For someone who wrote so movingly about the mystic journey, for Eliot not to have been a mystic himself must be because it was not God's grace that he should be.

12. Ibid., 142.
13. Ibid., 107.

Chapter 7

Dante

Beginning September 7, 1940, and lasting until May 1941, the German air force carried out daily bombing attacks against London in what became known as the "Blitz." In the initial raid alone 350 bombers flew from airfields in France across the Channel to drop hundreds of tons of bombs on the English. During these raids, which were in preparation for a German invasion of the British Isles (which never happened because Hitler preferred instead to invade the Soviet Union), much of London was destroyed and thousands were killed or injured. During the Blitz, Eliot served as an air raid warden or "fire watcher" stationed on a rooftop in South Kensington.

Lyndall Gordon, in her Eliot biography, describes the aftermath of what Eliot observed:

> [T]he accumulated debris would be suspended
> in the London air for hours and then would
> slowly descend, covering people in a fine, white ash.
> . . . He gazed down on a London much of which had turned
> into smouldering heaps of rubble. After a raid there
> would be an eerie silence. There was no traffic, since
> most of the streets were blocked by fallen buildings, and

hardly any pedestrians, only a pall of smoke, and every-
where an acrid smell of burning.[1]

For many there was a contemporary Blitz experience which
comes to mind. Remember the September 11, 2001 terrorist attacks on the World Trade Center buildings in New York City. Recall images of the first plane hitting one of the buildings; explosion,
fire, panic, uncertainty, fear of what might happen next. Then the
other plane crashing into the second building. More panic, disbe-
lief, anxiety, and fear. The buildings collapsed. We asked ourselves
how many would be killed or injured. Were loved ones at risk because they found themselves in New York City? Questions which
had no immediate answers because communication systems were
overloaded and didn't function. The streets were filled with people
hopefully fleeing to safety. Emergency workers responded; sirens
wailed. Tiny bits of paper clouded the sky and covered bodies,
making them appear ghost-like. Recalling that day, would you
have been in the mood to write poetry? Eliot was.

From his wartime experience Elliot was inspired to write a
scene which at the same time paid homage to his favorite poet,
Dante, and captured a vision of what he had experienced in the
Blitz. (Recall that the final three quartets, written between 1940
and 1942, were described by Eliot as the "Wartime Poems.") The
Blitz scene is in the second part of section II of "Little Gidding"
and opens "In the uncertain hour before the morning / Near
the ending of interminable night / At the recurrent end of the
unending."[2] After the air raid, the poet meets a stranger whom
Eliot identifies as a "familiar compound ghost." Eliot and the ghost
walk together ("trod the pavement in a dead patrol") and discuss
their mutual ideas of poetry. When the all-clear siren sounds, the
ghost disappears.

Eliot wrote that the inspiration for his Blitz scene was canto
XV of Dante's *Inferno*. In his 1950 lecture to the Italian Institute,
Eliot said he

1. Gordon, *T. S. Eliot*, 375.
2. Eliot, *Collected Poems*, 202.

wrote, in 'Little Gidding,' a passage which is intended to be the nearest equivalent to a canto of the *Inferno* or the *Purgatorio* in style as well as content, that I could achieve. The intention, of course, was the same as with my allusions to Dante in *The Waste Land*: to present to the mind of the reader a parallel, by means of contrast, between *Inferno* and *Purgatorio*, which Dante visited and a hallucinated scene after an air-raid."[3]

Before examining canto XV of the *Inferno*, attention should be given to Dante himself and *The Divine Comedy* (*The Comedia* in the orginal). Dante Alighieri was the greatest Italian poet to ever live. Eliot adopted such a superlative view ("highest point that poetry has ever reached").[4] Dante was born in Florence in May 1265, where he lived until his exile in 1302. He never returned to his native city and died in 1321. His exile was the result of being in the losing political party in a conflict between two factions of the Ghibelline party which ruled Florence (Dante was a member of the "white" party opposing the ruling "black" party). During his exile he wrote *The Comedia*, a long (over 14,000 lines) epic poem in three parts: *Inferno* (Hell), *Purgatorio*, and *Paradiso* (Heaven). The poem tells of Dante's journey, through three realms of the dead, but in a larger sense it is the spiritual journey of Dante to the Divine. *The Comedia* joins the Gita and *The Assent of Mount Carmel* in the spiritual journey to the Divine genre, along with the Quartets. Initially, Dante is guided by the greatest Roman poet Virgil (70 BCE-19 BCE), author of *The Aeneid*. Virgil was an obvious pick as a guide to the Underworld since in *The Aeneid* he had written about Aeneas making his own visit to that place. Toward the end of *Purgatorio*, a new guide replaces Virgil for the final assent to Heaven—Beatrice, a young Florentine women whom Dante had met as a young boy and admired from afar for many years. The story of this very complex and multi-layered poem can by summarized as follows: Dante on the night before Good Friday (April 7) in the year 1300 finds himself (in the middle of life at age

3. Eliot, *To Criticize the Critic and Other Writings*, 128.
4. Eliot, *Selected Essays*, 251.

35) lost in a dark wood. Virgil appears, having been sent from the Underworld by Beatrice who is already in Heaven, to guide Dante out of the woods and along a journey through the Inferno ("an eternal place where you shall hear the howls of desperation and see the ancient spirits in their pain")[5], Mount Purgatory ("those souls who are content within the fire, for they hope to reach . . . the blessed people")[6], and finally Paradise (Heaven), where Dante catches a glimpse of the face of God.

Eliot wrote two essays on Dante and in 1950 spoke about "What Dante Means To Me." In the 1950 lecture he said: "I still, after forty years, regard his poetry as the most persistent and deepest influence upon my own verse."[7] He included Dante among great masters like Shakespeare, Homer, and Virgil. Eliot acknowledged he had "borrowed lines from [Dante], in the attempt to reproduce, or rather arouse in the reader's mind the memory, of some Dantesque scene."[8]

In a 1929 essay Eliot wrote, "more can be learned about how to write poetry from Dante than from any English poet."[9] In particular he singled out the last canto of *Paradiso* as "the highest point that poetry has ever reached or ever can reach."[10] Staying with that last canto Eliot concludes, "Nowhere in poetry has experience so remote from ordinary experience been expressed so concretely, by a masterly use of imagery of light which is the form of certain types of mystical experience."[11] The "so remote from ordinary experience" was, of course, Dante's vision of the Divine. Eliot writes that Dante "could thus at every moment realize the inapprehensible in visual images."[12]

The final cantos in *Paradiso* illustrate the visual image of the inapprehensible Divine. Nevertheless, Dante prefaces his

---

5. Dante, *The Divine Comedy*, 62.

6. Ibid., 62.

7. Eliot, *To Criticize the Critic*, 125.

8. Ibid., 128.

9. Eliot, *Selected Essays*, 252.

10. Ibid., 251.

11. Ibid., 267.

12. Ibid., 269–70.

description with a disclaimer as to his ability to describe the Divine. Dante writes: "I saw things that he who from that height descends, forgets or can not speak; . . . our intellect sinks into an abyss so deep that memory fails to follow it."[13] In spite of that, he observes that all the elect who have attained Heaven are seated in a configuration in the shape of a white rose. Above the rose the Divine is seen as a "threefold Light" composed of three circles—two circles reflected against each other "as rainbow is by rainbow" and the third "fire breathed equally by those two circles." God is seen as light which "so penetrates the universe according to the worth of every part, that no thing can impede it."[14]

Eliot writes his own Dantesque scene in "Little Gidding," (section [IIb]) modeled on *Inferno* canto XV wherein Dante meets his former master and mentor, Brunetto Latini (1220–1294). Dante is walking along the top of an embankment and Brunetto is walking along the bank of a river in Hell. Brunetto grabs the hem of Dante's robe and says, "This is marvelous." To which Dante responds: "Are you here, Ser Brunetto?" Brunetto calls Dante "my son." They proceed to walk along the bank and discuss Florentine politics. Brunetto asserts that had he lived he would have supported Dante against his political enemies. Dante responds that if he had his way Brunetto would "still be among, not banished from humanity."[15] Dante adds he will always be grateful to Brunetto for teaching him "how man makes himself eternal."[16] Brunetto breaks off the conversation by asking Dante to "let my Tesoro, in which I still live, be precious to you."[17] Interestingly, the *Tesoro* contained a visit to the Underworld, so Dante had not only the example of an Underworld visit in the *The Aeneid*, but also the *Tesoro*.

Taking the scene in canto XV where Dante meets Brunetto Latini as a model, Eliot writes his own Dantesque scene ("Little Gidding," section II, lines 25–96) as follows: After the German

13. Dante, *The Divine Comedy*, 379.

14. Ibid., 527.

15. Ibid., 123.

16. Ibid., 123.

17. Ibid., 124.

planes ("dark dove with the flickering tongue" [machine gun]) have ended the attack and left the skies over London, leaving the leaves on trees rattling like tin, there was silence. The poet meets a man with "down-turned face" with "brown baked features" similar to Dante's description of Brunetto Latini, who is recognized as a "familiar compound ghost." In a very confusing passage, Eliot assumes a "double part" and not only speaks but hears another's voice ask "what, are you here?" in the same words Dante used in meeting Brunetto Latini in *Inferno*. Eliot knows himself but at the same time feels he is "someone other." The two proceed to walk the streets together. Who is the ghost? Eliot suggested in a letter to Eudo C. Mason in 1946 that it could be Yeats, Swift, Mallarme, or Poe. Regardless of who the ghost represents, Eliot asks the ghost to make a statement. The ghost declines to discuss his own "thought and theory" (which the ghost charges Eliot has already forgotten) but instead urges Eliot to forgive himself both good and bad in his own work. The past is over; one should move on. The ghost then discloses what he terms "the gifts reserved for age." First, expect that there will be loss of sense as one grows older. Second, there will be rage at human folly. Finally, there will be pain in remembering what we have done to others. The ghost concludes by saying that redemption from the gifts of age can be redeemed "by that refining fire / Where you must move in measure, like a dancer."[18] At the sound of the all-clear siren, the ghost leaves.

The "dark dove with the flickering tongue" which appears in the Blitz scene makes another appearance in section IV, but is transformed into the dove of the Holy Spirit (see Matthew 3:16). This time the dove is on fire and said to be the "one discharge from sin and error." Consequently, the choice for redemption is either the fire of the Holy Spirit or the fire of Hell. This choice between "pyre or pyre" is described as a "torment" and the question is posed: Who created this dilemma for man? The answer is love. George Herbert (1593–1633) was a favorite poet of Eliot and two Herbert poems may help to explain the assertion that God's love is the source of

---

18. Eliot, *Collected Poems*, 205.

mankind's choice to live with love or suffer the consequences of Divine judgement. In "Whitsunday" Herbert writes:

> Listen sweet Dove unto my song,
>> And spread thy golden wings in me:
>> Hatching my tender heart so long,
> Till it get wing, and fly away with thee.[19]

The dove is a symbol of God's love descending on mankind, and if one's heart is "hatched," then man can enter union with the Divine. The next stanza of the Herbert poem confirms that fire is an integral part of the experience of the dove descending "with flame of incandescent terror." Herbert writes: "Where is the fire which once descended / On the Apostles?"[20] Herbert's poem "Love" agrees that Love (God) is the source of the "intolerable shirt of flame / Which human power cannot remove."[21] He writes:

> Truth Lord, but I have marr'd them: let my shame
>> Go where it doth deserve.
> And know you not, says Love, who bore the blame?[22]

What has been "marr'd" are man's eyes as a result of unkindness and lack of gratitude; in other words, man's sin. The result is that man is not able to look at God. He is not able to enter into relationship with God. However, the response of God is that a relationship is sought and God, shockingly, takes responsibility for not only man's creation but also his sin.

Earlier, in "Burnt Norton" (III), Eliot had used the London subway as a substitute for Dante's *Inferno*. Here was "a place of disaffection . . .in a dim light." The subway riders had "strained time-ridden faces," and they were "distracted from distraction by distraction." Their apathetic minds were "filled with fancies and empty of meaning." There was a "cold wind that blows before and after time," which is unhealthy for the lungs. This unhealthy place of

19. Herbert, *The Complete English Works*, 57.

20. Ibid., 57.

21. Eliot, *Collected Poems*, 207.

22. Herbert, *The Complete English Works*, 184.

darkness is contrasted with the Darkness of God ("the world of per-petual solitude") which is part of the soul's journey to the Divine.[23]

In "East Coker" the poet is "in the middle way" much like Dante was in the opening canto of *Inferno* "when I [Dante] jour-neyed half of our life's way." Just as Dante was lost in the woods, Eliot found himself:

> In the middle, not only in the middle of the way
> But all the way, in a dark wood[24]

For both Dante and Eliot the way out of the dark woods is to continue on their spiritual journey to the Divine.

23. Eliot, *Collected Poems*, 178–79.
24. Ibid., 185.

Chapter 8

The Journey Began

1927

August	"Journey of the Magi"*
December	"Salutation" (will form part II of *Ash Wednesday*)

1928

Spring	"Because I Do Not Hope to Turn" (will form part I of *Ash-Wednesday*)
September	"A Song for Simeon"*

1929

October	"Animula"*
Autumn	"Som de L'Escalina" (will form Part III of *Ash Wednesday*)

1930

April	*Ash Wednesday* (including parts IV, V, and VII which were not published separately)
September	"Marina"*

1931

October	Triumphal March*

Ariel Poem

Forsaking his Unitarian upbringing, Eliot decided he wished to join the Church of England. He consulted his clergyman friend,

William Force Stead, as to the process for becoming an Anglican. Stead made the arrangements and, on June 29, 1927, Eliot was baptized by Stead in a private ceremony at Holy Trinity Church, Finstock, Oxfordshire. Confirmation immediately followed the next day with the Bishop of Oxford, Thomas Banks Strong, laying on his hands. There were only two witnesses, neither a family member. He did not immediately inform anyone, including his wife, of these events. In a letter to Stead, Eliot wrote "for the moment, it concerns me alone, & not the public—not even those nearest me."[1]

How baptism and confirmation changed his personal life is not our concern, but there was a profound impact on his poetry. Between 1927 and 1931, Eliot published eleven poems—five *Ariel Poems* and six poems which form *Ash Wednesday*. These eleven poems are not like any of his previous poetry. Just compare the title of his 1925 poem, "The Hollow Men," (the last published poem prior to his conversion) with the title of his first post-conversion poem, "The Journey of the Magi." Something significant had occurred in his life leading him to abandon the disillusionment, pessimism, and loss of faith in "The Hollow Men" as well as *The Waste Land*, and instead proceed to an examination of the spiritual life.

In order to judge the stark shift in the poetry between 1925 and 1927, treat "The Hollow Men" as the benchmark for comparison of Eliot's poetry beginning in 1927 (and for the rest of his life). "The Hollow Men" is a poem in five parts (each of the Quartets as well has five parts) which can be summarized as follows:

Part I—there are modern men who are literally stuffed with straw (they are scarecrows) and lead "quiet and meaningless" lives. They ask to be remembered by those who are permitted to enter "death's other kingdom" (see *Inferno* canto III).

Part II—these straw men avoid eye contact because eyes reveal truth and the men do not want to see truth or bear judgment at the end of life.

Part III—they live in a dead land and pray to dead stones, all the while wondering what life is like in "death's other kingdom."

1. Eliot and Haffenden, *The Letters of T. S. Eliot, Vol. 3*, 404.

Part IV—they are stranded and cannot save themselves; their only hope is intervention of the Divine ("multifoliate rose"—see *Paradiso* canto XXXIII) but they do not expect that to happen.

Part V—"the Shadow" prevents the men from acting and the poem ends with the men trying to sing a childhood nursery rhyme but the words are not known exactly and they attempt to pray but are not able to complete The Lord's Prayer accurately.

This is a poem of despair, hopelessness, loss of faith, loss of belief, and utter defeat. Eliot later called the poem "blasphemous" and wrote that "it stands for the lowest point I ever reached in my sordid domestic affairs."[2]

"JOURNEY OF THE MAGI"

Eliot's first poem following his conversion is "Journey of the Magi" which is also his first so-called *Ariel Poem*. A series of *Ariel Poems* were published by Faber (the publishing house of which Eliot was a director) between 1927 and 1931. Various poets contributed to the series; each poem was separately published in a small booket with original color artwork. Each book was wrapped in seasonal paper and was intended to serve as a substitute for Christmas cards. Eliot contributed to the series each year. When Faber discontinued the *Ariel Poems*, Eliot appropriated the title to designate four of his poems in his *Collected Poems, 1909–1935*. In 1954, Faber published a second series of *Ariel Poems*, including Eliot's "The Cultivation of Christmas Trees." No further *Ariel Poems* were published after 1954. The complete set of six poems by Eliot (including "Triumphal March") was published by Faber in 2014 as a separate volume (including original artwork from the earlier volumes).

Responding to a compliment from a friend about the poem, Eliot said he had no illusion about the poem and had written it quickly in less than an hour "with the assistance of half a bottle of

2. Ricks and McCue, *The Poems of T. S. Eliot, Vol. 1*, 714.

Booth's gin."[3] In spite of his cavalier attitude toward the poem, with this poem Eliot initiated the unifying theme for all the rest of his poetry (excluding *Old Possum's Book of Practical Cats*, published in 1939)—namely, the idea of incarnation, which defines the intersection of the Divine plane with the plane of man (see chapter 4) and is the central Christian belief. It is, of course, a paradox which cannot be explained rationally, but only alluded to in image and symbol. The opening lines of the poem (which describe how bad the weather was on the magi's journey to visit the birth of the Christ child) are quoted from the 1622 Christmas sermon preached by Lancelot Andrewes (see chapter 9) to King James I. The narrator of the poem remembers the cold journey in "[t]he very dead of winter" to visit Bethlehem. Numerous obstacles were encountered on the journey and overall a hard time was had. Throughout the journey the narrator and his companions questioned why they were even making the trip and whether the whole idea was folly. It was not easy to locate the place, but eventually the travelers did find the Christ child (incarnation). Rather than recalling the joy of that encounter, the magi questions the reason for making the journey; he finds a paradox –was it birth or death he witnessed? There was a birth for certain, but this birth was "[h]ard and bitter agony for us."[4] To the magi this birth seemed more like death and they were changed by the experience, "no longer at ease" in the ways before the journey. The poem ends with the magi disappointed and not being willing to embrace the new life possible because of the Incarnation. Clearly, this is not the typical Christmas story based on Mathew 2:1–12. What is learned about the spiritual journey from the first *Ariel Poem* is that encountering the Divine can leave us "no longer at ease."

The idea that incarnation presents the possibility of both birth and death is repeated in the Interlude between Act I and Act II of Eliot's play *Murder in the Cathedral*. Eliot had been commissioned to write a play for the Canterbury Festival of 1935. The play was staged in the cathedral Chapter House before transferring to a London

3. Eliot and Haffenden, *The Letters of T. S. Eliot, Vol.* 3, 700.

4. Eliot, *Collected Poems*, 100.

theatre. The Interlude is a fictional sermon preached by the principal character, Thomas Beckett, archbishop of Canterbury, on Christmas morning, 1170. The sermon foretells Beckett's martyrdom which takes place in Act II. In the sermon, Becket reminds his listeners that the celebration of Christmas should remind them of not only the birth of Christ but also his martyrdom. Thus, there is both joy and mourning at once at the Incarnation similar to the experience of the magi at the birth of Christ. As a set the *Ariel Poems* address the questions of how does one approach the possibility of transformation (new life), and what is the reaction to the experience?

"SALUTATION"

(*Ash Wednesday* II)

"Salutation" (original title for the poem later renamed "Lady, three white leopards sat under a juniper tree") was the first part written in what was to eventually become a six-part work titled *Ash Wednesday*. Although written first "Salutation" would be placed as part II of the final grouping of poems. *Ash Wednesday* is often referred to as Eliot's "conversion poem" as it was completed in 1930, three years after his reception into the Church of England. Eliot explained that the poem was intended to describe "the experience of a man in search of God and trying to explain to himself his intenser human feelings in terms of the divine goal."[5] Earlier he had written that *Ash Wednesday* was "merely an attempt to put down in words a certain stage of the journey, a journey of which I insist that all my previous verse represents previous stages."[6] In terms of the spiritual journey discussed in chapter 5, *Ash Wednesday* seems to represent the stage in the journey known as "purgation" in which penance and renunciation prepare the soul for further stages in the journey to the Divine. *Ash Wednesday* is not the realization of that sought-after goal which will finally be addressed twelve years hence in "Little Gidding."

---

5. Eliot and Haffenden, *The Letters of T. S. Eliot, Vol.* 5, 288.

6. Ibid., 199.

"Salutation" opens with a startling allegory of a lady in a white gown sitting next to three white leopards under a tree, the leopards having fed on the body of the poet. Only the bones and indigestible parts of the body are left. In the tradition of devouring myths the hero is swallowed and then transformed. The Biblical story of Jonah is an example. An even more pertinent analog is the restoration oracle in Ezekiel 37:1–14. In the Valley of the Dry Bones a prophet is shown a countless number of bones, and instructed to prophesy to the dry bones that God will renew the bones with sinew, flesh, and skin so that the bones will be reconstituted as human beings. This story is a metaphor for Israel during its Babylonian exile (587 BCE) and promised that God would give new life to the people of Israel and restore them to their lands. The bones in "Salutation" are symbolic of the poet's renunciation of ego ("Proffer my deeds to oblivion, and my love / To the posterity of the desert and the fruit of the gourd,"[7] [e.g., death, see Jonah 4]). There will be no reconstituted body, but the former life will be forgotten and instead the poet will be henceforth "devoted, concentrated in purpose."[8] That new purpose is the Rose which "is now the Garden / Where all loves end."[9] This transformation is mediated by a good and beautiful "lady of silences" who "withdraws" to contemplate the Virgin Mary. The "single Rose / Is now the Garden"[10] seems to allude to the culminating symbol of the Divine in the conclusion of Dante's *Paradiso* (cantos XXX and XXXI). There are other gardens in which man meets God, namely the Garden of Eden (Genesis 2:7–9), the garden of Augustine's conversion (*The Confessions of St. Augustine*, chapters 8–12), and most important to our purpose, the rose garden of "Burnt Norton" where the poet first experiences the "Aha" moment ("Awaking"). The poem concludes with the poet accepting the loss of ego ("We are glad to be scattered, we did little good to each other") and "united / in the quiet of the desert."[11]

7. Eliot, *Collected Poems*, 87.

8. Ibid., 87.

9. Ibid., 88.

10. Ibid., 88.

11. Ibid., 88.

There is a final reference to God's inheritance in Ezekiel 48:29 ("This is the land which ye / Shall divide by lot") of the Promised Land where God will be present. The poet too seems content with the spiritual rebirth experienced following renunciation of the ego. It should be noted that the Lady of Silence's intervention is an act of grace in assisting the poet in dying to self (ego).

What do we make of the three white leopards? What symbolism did Eliot intend? Initially he rejected any reference point at all. "But if the three leopards . . . contain any allusion literary, I don't know what they are. Can't I sometimes invent nonsense, instead of always being supposed to borrow it?"[12] Nevertheless, later that year, Eliot wrote to Peter Monro Jack, "You are the only person who has so to speak, spotted the White Leopards as The World, The Flesh and the Devil . . ."[13] Given Eliot's fondness for Dante's *The Divine Comedy* it has been suggested that the leopards are really an allusion to the leopard, wolf, and lion who block Dante's assent to Paradise and force him to pursue an alternate route through Hell and Purgatory. Whatever the actual source, the white leopards, in spite of devouring the poet, seem to be harmless and beautiful (white as a liturgical color symbolizes purity, holiness, and virtue—used for High Holy Days of the church year, especially Christmas and Easter).

"ALL ABOARD FOR NATCHEZ, CAIRO AND ST. LOUIS"

(*Ash Wednesday* I)

This unusual title for the poem is the opening line of a song on one of Eliot's favorite records ("The Early Bird Catches the Worm," 1927). The cities mentioned are stops along the way for a steamboat making its way from New Orleans to St. Louis. It is not clear what Eliot had in mind when he assigned this title to the poem when it was separately published before its later incorporation into *Ash*

12. Eliot and Haffenden, *The Letters of T. S. Eliot, Vol.* 5, 197.

13. Ibid., 434.

Wednesday. Eliot was a borrower of titles, lines, and whatever from the works of other authors and this poem contains several examples. The first line ("Because I do not hope to turn again")[14] comes from a poem by Guido Cavalcanti (1255–1300) who was a contemporary of Dante. In line 4, Eliot borrows a line from Shakespeare's Sonnet 29 ("Desiring this man's art, and that man's scope . . . ")[15] and alters it to read "Desiring this man's gift and that man's scope".[16]

The most significant borrowing in the poem is from the sixteenth-century Spanish mystic John of the Cross. In his work *The Ascent of Mount Carmel/The Dark Night,* John of the Cross adopts a metaphor which he called the "Dark Night" to designate the path leading to union with God. In the initial stage of the Dark Night the pilgrim is called on to mortify the appetites and deny the pleasure of all things. John of the Cross wrote:

> The necessity of passing through this dark night
> (the mortification of the appetites and the denial
> of pleasure in all things) for the attainment of the
> divine union with God arises from the fact that
> all of man's attachments to creatures are pure
> darkness in God's sight. Clothed in these affections,
> a person will be incapable of the enlightenment
> and dominating fullness of God's pure and
> simple light, unless he rejects them.[17]

Thus, the poet has begun his journey in the Dark Night and does not "hope to turn again" (that is, to turn away from and reject the journey to God). He therefore renounces and detaches himself from a number of things:

- "this man's gift and that man's scope"
- "power of the usual reign"

---

14. Eliot, *Collected Poems,* 85.

15. Shakespeare, *The Riverside Shakespeare,* 1848.

16. Eliot, *Collected Poems,* 85.

17. John of the Cross, *Collected Works,* 77–78.

- "glory of the positive hour"
- "transitory power"
- a garden "where trees flower, and springs flow"
- "the blessed face"[18]

Following these specific renunciations the poet is left "to construct something / Upon which to rejoice."[19]

Before proceeding to attempt to construct anything the poet prays for God's mercy and help to truly forget those matters which have been renounced. There is an acknowledgement that the poet lacks the capacity on his own to move forward in the Dark Night ("wings are no longer wings to fly / But merely vans ["wings"] to beat the air").[20] He asks for the gift of stillness which has a Biblical basis: "Be still and know that I am God" (Psalm 46:10); "In stillness and quiet there lies my strength" (Isaiah 30:15). The importance of the "still point" in *Four Quartets* is discussed in chapter 4. The poem concludes with the poet praying The Hail Mary ("Holy Mary, Mother of God, pray for us sinners now and at the hour of our death"), but without the poet constructing "something / Upon which to rejoice."

"A SONG FOR SIMEON"

The second *Ariel Poem* makes the point that the transformation and new life offered by the Incarnation will not be embraced by everyone. The story of Simeon as told by Eliot in "A Song for Simeon" illustrates rejection of the new life. The story is roughly based on Luke 2:22–25. As required by Hebrew law the infant Jesus was taken to the temple in Jerusalem and a sacrifice made of a pair of doves. An elderly man (Eliot makes him eighty in the poem) by the name of Simeon was hoping for the restoration of Israel and believed he would not die until he had seen the Messiah. While in the temple when Mary and Joseph presented the child, Simeon recognized the

18. Eliot, *Collected Poems*, 85.
19. Ibid., 85.
20. Ibid., 86.

Christ and said that having seen the Christ child he was prepared to die. Moreover, he told Mary the mother of Jesus, her son would be rejected and Mary herself would be "pierced to the heart." Many others in Israel would stand or fall because of Jesus. Luke's version of the Simeon story would later form the basis for a prayer known as the "*Nunc dimittis*" in *The Book of Common Prayer*:

> Lord, now lettest thou thy servant depart in
> peace according to thy word;
> For mine eyes have seen thy salvation,
> which thou has prepared before the
> face of all people
> To be a light to lighten the Gentiles, and
> to be the glory of thy people Israel.[21]

In Eliot's rendering of the story the locale may have shifted from Jerusalem to Rome ("Roman hyacinths"). Simeon is waiting for death. He says that he is a good man who has kept the faith and fed the poor. Nevertheless, he worries that his children will flee "the time of sorrow." He predicts the Jewish Diaspora in which his children will be forced to flee "from the foreign faces and foreign words." Before that happens he prays he may be granted peace and essentially left alone to die. Simeon rejects martyrdom, the ecstasy of thought and prayer, and union with the Divine ("the ultimate vision"). He is tired of not only his life but also the lives of his children. Surprisingly, even though he has seen "thy salvation" (the Incarnation) his plea is to "leave me alone. I want to die." Like Simeon in Luke's account, Eliot's Simeon recognizes the Christ Child ("unspeaking and unspoken Word"), but unlike Luke's Simeon, Eliot's Simeon rejects the possibility of transformation and new life—he is unable to move to a new order as a result of incarnation. There is a choice to be made; the Divine is accessible to man, but whether to embrace the spiritual journey is left up to man.[22]

---

21. *The Book of Common Prayer*, 120.

22. Eliot, *Collected Poems*, 101–02.

"ANIMULA"

Continuing the theme that man operates with free will and is not forced to accept transformation and new life as a result of incarnation, Eliot's third *Ariel Poem*, "Animula," addresses the question whether the soul is naturally drawn to God. His answer is generally no.

The poem begins with references to two rather obscure poems from antiquity. First, the title of the poem is taken from a poem by the Roman Emperor Hadrian. As he lay dying in 138 AD he dictated verses to his soul and the first word in his poem was "animula" ("Animula vagula, blandula . . .")[23] meaning "little soul" or "simple soul." Second, Eliot's poem itself tracks Dante's *Purgatorio* canto XVI. As Dante makes his way upward through Pugatory, he meets Marco Lombard, an Italian courtier who lived in the thirteenth century, and Dante asks Marco why there is evil in the world. Is evil caused by the planets and the stars as some astrologers say or by mankind? Marco replies that if the heavens controlled what man does then there would be no free will and "there would be no equity in joy for doing good, in grief for evil."[24] Marco argues that to say the stars control human action is to deny the freedom of human will to choose between good and evil. No, it is not the stars which dictate, but humans who choose to do evil. Marco then proceeds to set forth his notion of the "simple soul." From the hand of God there issues the simple soul who at birth is innocent, but easily attracted to trivial things which bring delight but not to God. To prevent the soul from turning to trivial things the spiritual law is necessary to guide the soul's conduct. Even though the law is present to guide mankind there is still evil in the world because the law is not enforced due to bad leadership of the Roman Church.

Following closely the scene with Dante and Marco, Eliot begins his poem with a quotation from canto XVI—"Issues from the hand of God, the simple soul."[25] The soul is pictured as an infant

23. Ricks and McCue, *The Annotated Poems, Vol.* 1, 769.

24. Dante, *The Divine Comedy*, 290.

25. Eliot, *Collected Poems*, 103.

crawling between the legs of tables and chairs and playing with toys. Keeping with the Christmas theme of the *Ariel Poems,* Eliot notes the child's pleasure in a Christmas tree. Other delights of the child are noted—sunlit patterns on the floor, the design on a silver tray and playing cards. But the soul does not remain simple; the growing soul finds burdens and complexities, imperatives and control. There is pain in living, forcing the small soul to retreat into knowledge ("Curl up . . . Behind the Encyclopaedia Britannica").[26] As the soul progresses over time it becomes irresolute, selfish, misshapen, lame, immobile, fearing the good. There does not appear to be any happy resolution of this situation as described in the poem until after the viaticum. The viaticum is the Eucharist given immediately before death. The resolution offered by the poem seems to be that because the soul is not naturally drawn to God, transformation does not come as part of normal human development but instead can only come through the intervention of God's grace. In spite of the pessimism of the poem it ends with the request to "Pray for us now and at the hour of our birth."[27] Note that the word "birth" is a substitution for the word "death" in this line from the prayer known as "Ave Maria." The substitution seems appropriate in context of the poem because prayer is needed at the beginning of life in order to avoid the corruption of the simple soul as described in the poem. Moreover, there is a tendency for Eliot to interchange "birth" and "death" in his work (see "Journey of the Magi" where the narrator is not sure he witnessed a birth or a death, and Becket's sermon in *Murder in the Cathedral).*

(In the final six lines of the poem there are specific names for whom prayers are requested—Guiterriez, Boudin, and Floret. Eliot has said that he did not intend for these names to be actual persons.)

---

26. Ibid., 103.
27. Ibid., 104.

"SOM DE L'ESCALINA"

(*Ash Wednesday* III)

"Som de l'esalina" ("the summit of the stair"), the original title of the poem which became part III of *Ash Wednesday*, is a phrase from the words spoken to Dante by Arnaut Daniel in *Purgatorio* canto XXVI:

> Now, by the Power that conducts you to
> the summit of the stairway, I pray you:
> remember, at the time opportune, my pain![28]

A stair (or ladder) is a metaphor for the ascent to a new life and has been used numerous times to describe the journey to God. For example, in Genesis 28 Jacob in a dream "saw a ladder, which rested on the ground with its top reaching to heaven." In the poem which is explicated at great length in *The Ascent of Mount Carmel*, John of the Cross writes, "In darkness and secure / By the secret ladder, disguised."[29] This secret ladder leads to God in the same manner as Jacob's ladder.

The poet has an out-of-body experience as he ascends the stair; at the first turning of the second stair he is able to look back to see himself ("The same shape twisted") struggling with the Devil who with deceitful hope and despair is trying to prevent the poet from ascending the stair. The poet, however, is able to keep climbing. Then at the first turning of the third stair he looks out a window to see a "broadbacked figure drest in blue and green"[30] playing the flute and serenading a lady with brown hair. Although not more specifically identified, this flute player resembles Pan, the pagan god of sexual perversion. He represents the lower or animal side of man. If this figure is Pan, he is likely serenading the lady trying to seduce her. Although the scene is attractive to the poet and probably reminds him of something in his past, he is able to reject (the image

---

28. Dante, *The Divine Comedy*, 340.
29. John of the Cross, *Complete Works*, 68.
30. Eliot, *Collected Poems*, 89.

is "Fading, fading") the temptation to stop his ascent and return to his former life (see parts I and II of *Ash Wednesday*). He finds the strength "beyond hope and despair" to keep climbing.

Once again the poem closes with a prayer—"Lord, I am not worthy." But like the centurion in Matthew 8:8 ("The centurion answered and said, Lord, I am not worthy that thou shouldest come under my roof: but speak the word only, and my servant shall be healed.") even though the poet finds himself to be unworthy he has the faith to ask that the word be spoken ("but speak the word only"). Jesus found the centurion to have great faith and the implication is that the poet too has faith.

"WHO WALKED BETWEEN THE VIOLET AND THE VIOLET"

(*Ash Wednesday* IV)

"Who walked between the violet and the violet" is a surprising departure from the first three parts of *Ash Wednesday*. There is no "I" indicating the poet speaking so there is no self-reflection by the poet and renunciation of past deeds. Instead there are bizarre and wonderful visual images of "jeweled unicorns," "fiddles and flutes," and "sand / In the blue of larkspur." It may even be the intended climax of the entire six-part work. Eliot does however, provide a clue in the twentieth line for getting at the poem's meaning: "The unread vision in the higher dream." That clue of the higher dream leads to Eliot's essay on Dante, wherein Eliot draws a distinction between the "low dream" and the "high dream," or vision.[31] Taking examples from *The Divine Comedy* Eliot wrote:

> Dante's is a visual imagination. It is a visual imagination in a different sense from that of a modern painter of still life: it is visual in the sense that he lived in an age in which men still saw visions. It was a psychological habit, the trick of which we have forgotten, but as good as any of our own. We have nothing but dreams, and we have

31. Ibid., 90.

forgotten that seeing visions—a practice now relegated
to the aberrant and uneducated—was once a more significant, interesting, and disciplined kind of dreaming.[32]

This mental habit "which when raised to the point of genius
can make a great poet as well as a great mystic or saint."[33]

Dante's habit of dreaming the high dream and translating the
dream into his poetry is illustrated by Eliot in his discussion of
the divine pageant in cantos XXVIII-XXX of *Purgatorio*. In these
cantos Dante arrives in the Earthly Paradise, the Garden of Eden,
and encounters a heavenly pageant including among other things
seven golden candlesticks, four animals (described in Ezekiel),
and a chariot drawn by a griffin. When the pageant halts he meets
Beatrice, "a woman showed herself to me; above a white veil, she
was crowned with olive boughs; her cape was green; her dress
beneath, flame-red."[34] Beatrice, of course, will be Dante's guide to
Heaven. This pageant Eliot writes "belongs to the world of what I
call the high dream, and the modern world seems capable only of
the low dream."[35]

In "Who walked between the violet and the violet," Eliot writes
his own high dream in the manner of Dante as quoted above. The
poem opens with a lady dressed in white and blue, "Mary's colour,"
walking in a garden, which she has apparently created ("who then
made strong the fountains and made fresh the springs").She walks
among the violet flowers and talks about things without sorrow or
grief ("eternal dolour"). There are others in the garden but they are
not identified. The reader is urged to be mindful ("*sovegna vos*").
This garden (or dream) is a place where redemption can take place:
"bearing / Away the fiddles and flutes, restoring / One who moves in
the time between sleep and waking [the time when the high dream
occurs] . . . " Redemption comes about through tears and "a new
verse the ancient rhyme" in the "unread vision in the higher dream."
Similar to Dante's chariot drawn by a griffin, Eliot dreams "jeweled

32. Eliot, *Selected Essays*, 243.

33. Ibid., 243.

34. Dante, *The Divine Comedy*, 357.

35. Eliot, *Selected Essays*, 262.

unicorns draw by the gilded hearse." The lady speaks in the opening part of the poem but falls silent toward the end to become the "silent sister." She stands between the yew trees (a tree associated with cemeteries and thus death) and the garden god (presumably Pan, see "Som de L'Escalina" above) who is unexpectedly silent as well ("whose flute is breathless"). In spite of the silence, the garden remains, a fountain flows, a bird sings—a symbol of redemption. It is a "token of the word, unheard, unspoken" until the "wind shake a thousand whispers from the yew. This token, nevertheless, is effective to restore new life (see Ezekiel 37:9, "Let winds come from every quarter and breathe into these slain, that they may come to life"—said over the dry bones, [see "Salutation" above]). Once the dream is over there is exile from the garden (dream). The words "our exile" are taken from the prayer "Salve Regina" (a prayer following celebration of the Mass, e.g., "turn, then, most gracious advocate, thine eyes of mercy toward us; and after this our exile, show unto us the blessed fruit of thy womb, Jesus").[36]

"IF THE LOST WORD IS LOST, IF THE SPENT WORD IS SPENT"

(Ash Wednesday V)

There may never have been a poem in which, in order to understand the meaning, it is necessary to carefully read noting whether "word" is spelled with a capital "W" or a lowercase "w." In the first fourteen lines of the poem this particular word appears twelve times—five times capitalized, seven times lowercased. When spelled in the latter manner we can be sure the normal dictionary meaning of "word" applies ("a speech sound, or series of such sounds, serving to communicate meaning").[37] But if spelled in the former manner and read by one who is familiar with Christian theology, then all bets are off because now we're dealing with the eternal word of God made incarnate in Jesus Christ (Gospel of

36. Eliot, *Collected Poems*, 90.
37. *Webster's New World College Dictionary*, 5th ed., 1666.

John 1:1), the Incarnation. As discussed elsewhere in this book, the Incarnation is the focus of all of Eliot's post-conversion poetry. With this understanding of the separate meanings of "word" we can explore the poem's meditation on word-Word.

Words can be lost, spent, unheard, and even unspoken. An "unspoken word" can be "still" in the sense of being unmoving, not drawing a response. Even the Word (incarnation) can be not moving ("still") if not heard or not eliciting a response. Nevertheless, the Word is always present in the world ("within / The world and for the world").To emphasize what the Word is, Eliot inserts a line from John 1:5 ("And the light shone in darkness"). A following line in John 1:5 is not quoted in the poem ("the darkness has never mastered it"), but the idea is present in the poem that the Word is always present in the world and has not been overcome ("Against the Word the unstilled world still whirled / About the center of the silent Word"). Carl Jung (1875–1961), the Swiss psychiatrist, captured this idea in the words etched over his fireplace: "Bidden or not bidden God is present." In spite of its presence in the world, the "Word" is not always "bidden." This point is made in the line "O my people, what have I done unto thee." (Micah 6:3) In this passage from Micah, God states his charge against Israel for disobedience in spite of all the great things God has done for the people. Similarly the poem indicts those who have heard the Word but it has not resonated with them. This failure of the Word to resound is explained by "there is not enough silence."[38]

Following this meditation on word-Word, the poem focuses on "those who walk in darkness," (Isaiah 9:2) those who have not seen the light of the Word. The veiled sister (presumably the same veiled sister from part IV) is asked to pray for those who:

- walk or wait in darkness
- chose thee and oppose thee
- are torn on the horn between season and season
- offend the veiled sister

38. Eliot, *Collected Poems*, 92–93.

- are children at the gate who can't leave and can't pray

- are terrified and cannot surrender

- affirm yet deny

The poem ends with a repeat of God's lament to the unfaithful people of Israel, "O my people."

"ALTHOUGH I DO NOT HOPE TO TURN AGAIN"

(*Ash Wednesday* VI)

The sixth and last section of *Ash Wednesday* almost reprises the opening of section I but with an important variation—instead of "Because I do not hope to turn again" the sixth section begins with "Although I do not hope to turn again." The word "although" seems weaker than the more intentional word "because." In section I the poet has made a choice not to turn again (from the Divine), but in section VI he is not so sure he will not turn again rejecting the Divine. He waivers and confesses he does "not wish to wish these things." In the words of the Roman Catholic confessional he asks for forgiveness ("Bless me father" [for I have sinned]). Try as he may the poet is not able to renounce the beautiful world he sees from his window—the granite shore, white sails, lilacs, goldenrod, the sea, quail, and plover. There is tension in life ("between dying and birth"). The poet is seeking the Divine, but remains time-bound. He is unable to renounce the world. All he can do is recognize he is in a place of solitude. The Virgin is not present but blue (the Virgin's color) rocks remind him of her spirit. So he prays to the blessed sister (from section IV) and the holy mother, whose spirit inhabits the garden and the fountain.[39]

He repeats words prayed in section I:

Teach us to care and not to care
Teach us to sit still[40]

39. Ibid., 94–95.
40. Ibid., 95.

These words invoke the approach to the Divine of apophatic mysticism or the "Via Negativa" (see chapter 5). These themes of stillness and not caring are returned to in "East Coker." ("I said to my soul, be still, and let the dark come upon you / which shall be the darkness of God. . . . I said to my soul, be still, and wait without hope.")[41] By repeating this prayer it seems that the poet has still not been able to enter the "Via Negativa" of silence, not hoping, simply waiting for God. There is no sense of resolution, but only continuing to go forward on the spiritual journey (this theme of boldly going forward will be addressed in "The Dry Salvages").

The poem ends with three prayers which reflect the poet's desire to continue on the journey to God. First, "Our peace is His will" is taken from Dante's *Paradiso* canto III, in which Dante asks Piccarda Donati, the sister of his friend, whether she desires a higher place in heaven so to be nearer to God. She replies no because she has been assigned her place by God and "in His will there is our peace." Second, "Suffer me not to be separated [from thee]" is from the medieval prayer known as "Anima Christi" ("Soul of Christ"). The prayer has been erroneously attributed to St. Ignatius Loyola, but the prayer has been found in manuscripts written before his birth. Last, "And let my cry come unto Thee" is taken from Psalm 102 ("Lord, hear my prayer and let my cry for help come to you.")[42]

At the end of *Ash Wednesday* the poet has hope for the spiritual journey, but is left without a clear glimpse of possible union with God. *Ash Wednesday* points toward a journey to incarnation which will be fully explored in *Four Quartets*. The poet has awakened to hints of the Divine and attempted without success to renounce (purgation) those things which are obstacles to meeting the Divine. The poet prays for strength "to sit still" and "to care and not to care;" he prays that by God's grace he will be able to travel the "Via Negativa." All of this is preparation for the spiritual journey which is the subject of *Four Quartets*.

41. Ibid., 186.
42. Ibid., 95.

"MARINA"

"Marina" is the most optimistic and celebratory of the *Ariel Poems*. Finally, a transformed life is recognized and fully embraced. However, before reaching that happy conclusion the poem juxtaposes death (in the form of the reference to the first-century play *Hercules Furens* [*The Madness of Hercules*], by the Roman playwright Seneca by the quotation in the epigraph) and life (in the form of allusions to Shakespeare's play *Pericles,* as well as the poem's title taken from the name of Pericles' lost daughter in the play). Both plays contain a so-called "recognition scene" except Hercules wakes to find he has slain his wife and children and Pericles wakes to find his lost child alive.

The Latin epigraph in the poem (*"Quis hic locus, quae regio, quae mundi plaga?"* which can be translated "What place is this, what region, what quarter of the world?") are the words spoken by Hercules upon waking to discover that he has killed his wife and children. Hercules, under a spell of madness brought on him by Juno, kills his family and immediately falls into a deep sleep. When he awakes and is no longer insane he tries to place himself and speaks the words in the epigraph. Gradually, he recognizes the horror of what he has done and considers his own suicide (he is persuaded by a friend not to take his own life).

In Shakespeare's play, Pericles and his wife, Thaisa, are on a sea journey to Tyre. During a storm Thaisa gives birth to a daughter they name Marina. Thaisa is believed to die in childbirth and her body is sealed in a watertight coffin and buried at sea. In fact the coffin washes ashore, Thaisa is discovered and revived (but that is another story). Believing his wife to be dead, Pericles goes to Tarsus where he entrusts the care of his infant daughter to friends. He then continues on to Tyre where he lives for the next sixteen years without bothering to reclaim Marina. On a visit to Tarsus Pericles learns that Marina has died. Actually, however, Marina has not died and is living in Mitylene. While deeply distressed at the loss of his daughter, Pericles visits Mitylene where he encounters Marina whom he does not initially recognize. After talking for awhile Pericles recognizes his lost daughter, and there is a happy reunion. Pericles had experienced the emotion of thinking Marina was dead, but then realizes the joy of the unexpected presence of life; Marina lives.

In "Marina," Eliot uses both recognition scenes discussed above to construct his poem. In the opening lines of the poem the allusion is to Hercules awaking from insanity to consciousness not knowing what he had done or even where he is. In the poem the speaker (counterpart to Hercules) asks a series of locating questions ("what seas what shores . . . "). Keeping with the theme that Hercules awakes to the realization he had killed his family, the next section of the poem emphasizes that death results from sin; four of the seven deadly sins are mentioned (gluttony, pride, sloth, and lust, but anger, envy, and ambition are omitted). In a pivot to the Pericles story, the deadly sins are said to become "unsubstantial . . . By this grace dissolved in place." This grace is realized through the speaker's vision of Marina, his lost daughter ("this face"). Gradually as her face becomes clearer she becomes the personification of hope to the speaker (the stand-in for Pericles in the poem). With this new hope the speaker sees the possibility of new life ("Living to live in a world of time beyond me", e.g., the vertical plane of transcendence [see chapter 4]).

Carl Jung has written that realization of a spiritual experience is often accompanied in dreams by a child figure who symbolizes the potential for transformation and new life. Marina fulfills that role for the speaker. Another Jungian concept which helps explain the poem is the boat which the speaker recalls immediately after his recognition of Marina. In dreams, a boat may be the association with a method or way of transformation. The speaker recalls a boat he had built while "unknowing, half conscious, unknown." Nevertheless, he takes responsibility (as "my own") for his boat that represents his previous life. The boat's present condition (speaker's life) is in a state of disrepair (bowsprit [a spar (sail) extending forward from the vessel's prow] and paint cracked, weak rigging, and rotten canvas).

Recognition of Marina ("this face") opens up the hope of new life which the speaker accepts ("let me / Resign my life for this life").[43] There is the hope for a new ship to replace the one with leaks and is in need of caulking. The poem ends with a series of locating questions similar to the opening lines of the poem, but the "what" here is not an inquiry but an expression of anticipation, even delight. The transformation to new life is merely begun and remains to be negotiated "through the fog." The hope of transformation and new life have been brought about by the experience of finding "my daughter," just as Pericles found his Marina after a sixteen-year separation.

This poem especially, but all of the *Ariel Poems* to some extent, show the first step in the spiritual journey which is the "awaking" to the presence of the Divine in the plane of man (see chapter 4). Anticipating "Burnt Norton," which he will write five years in the future, Eliot introduces several symbols of the presence of the Divine. First, there is the bird, a woodthrush in the poem. In "Burnt Norton" the bird is simply a thrush (after the encounter with the Divine the bird says "Go, go, go" because "human kind / Cannot bear very much reality").[44] Both poems have children laughing in the leaves. After the recognition of "this face" there is "small laughter between leaves and hurrying feet." In "Burnt Norton" "the leaves were full of children, / Hidden excitedly, containing laughter."[45]

"TRIUMPHAL MARCH"

The fifth and final *Ariel Poem* (putting aside a new series of *Ariel Poems*, published in 1954, which included Eliot's poem "The Cultivation of Christmas Trees," which would be the sixth and final *Ariel Poem* written by Eliot) was not published under the heading of "Ariel Poems" in Eliot's *Collected Poems, 1909-1935*. In spite of being separately published as an *Ariel Poem*, the poem "Triumphal March" was included under a section entitled "Unfinished Poems" as one of two parts of a work entitled "Coriolan." The poem takes

---

43. Ibid., 106.
44. Ibid., 176.
45. Ibid., 176.

the form of a spectator describing a Roman triumphal march in which a victorious general marches into Rome with his army and the spoils of war. Included is a precise inventory of the captured equipment paraded before the citizens of Rome, e.g., 5,800,000 rifles and carbines, 102,000 machine guns, etc. There is, however, a twist. Instead of a victorious general being the focus of attention, there is an unidentified "he" who is the center of attention. This person is described as "quiet" without "interrogation in his eyes." Nevertheless, his eyes are "watchful, waiting, perceiving, indifferent." Not recognized by the spectator-narrator of the poem is that this "he" is "the still point of the turning world"—a phrase which will re-appear in "Burnt Norton" and *Murder in the Cathedral* (Part I, Thomas' first speech, and later by the Fourth Tempter). As discussed in chapter 4, the Divine is present at the still point, but the spectator in the poem fails to see the Divine present in the march. All the spectator could see were many eagles (the standard of a Roman legion), trumpets, flags, and "stone, bronze, stone, steel, stone, oakleaves, horses' heels." At the conclusion of the parade the spectator asks for a light for his cigarette. He totally misses the "light" which incarnation offers to mankind. The fact that soldiers line the streets along the parade route is the spectator's final interest in the whole event. Eliot's point seems to be that getting lost in the triumphalism of the march may lead us to miss an encounter with the Divine. Seeking a "light" for one's cigarette is a trivial act compared to seeking the "light" of incarnation. We should be more watchful Eliot is telling us.[46]

SUMMARY

While the *Ariel Poems* and *Ash Wednesday* adumbrate elements of the spiritual journey, it is not until *Four Quartets* that the five stages of the mystic way are fully fleshed out by Eliot. Nevertheless, the earlier poems offer "hints and guesses" about the journey to incarnation.

46. Ibid., 125–26.

First and foremost, the earlier poems ("Journey of the Magi" and " A Song for Simeon") express no doubt that the Divine has entered on the plane of time (see chapter 4). The vertical plane of the Divine ("timelessness") intersects with the horizontal plane of man ("time"). Of that intersection there is not the slightest hesitation or doubt on the part of the poet. Mankind, on the other hand, is not by nature drawn to or disposed to embrace or even recognize the Divine intervention ("Animula"). Indeed, recognition may itself be a gift of Divine grace ("Suffer me not to be separated").[47] However, that recognition itself does not come naturally and is never automatic. Mankind has the freewill to reject a spiritual journey and ignore the Divine entirely ("A Song for Simeon"). Even if undertaken, the journey is never completely resolved because there may be "turns" followed by rejection, only to "turn" again (*Ash Wednesday*).

Encountering the Divine presents a paradox in that it may be life or death that is realized ("Journey of the Magi"). Thus, the encounter may be very unsettling ("no longer at ease here"). Moreover, the journey requires a heavy price: renunciation of prized things and persons as well as surrender of the ego (*Ash Wednesday*). Alertness is required (*sovegna vos,* meaning "be mindful") lest we miss seeing the intersection (incarnation) of the planes ("Triumphal March"). A key to being mindful is the cultivation of "stillness"—silence and waiting ("Teach us to sit still"). Even at the preliminary stages of the spiritual journey there is clearly hope on the part of the pilgrim seeking encounter (union) with the Divine ("Marina"). As seen later in "Burnt Norton" the initial encounter with the Divine ("aha") may take place in a garden (*Ash Wednesday*). There may be a guide or mediator or mediatrix ("veiled sister") assisting the pilgrim on her or his way.

In terms of the five stages of the mystic way (see chapter 5) the *Ariel Poems* and *Ash Wednesday* can be read to address the first three stages of the journey—awaking ("aha"), purgation, and the Dark Night. It is left to *Four Quartets* to address the final stages of illumination and union with the Divine.

47. Ibid., 95.

The *Ariel Poems* and *Ash Wednesday* describe the poet's conflicted, initial desire for the Divine, but the journey clearly has begun. *Four Quartets* will describe the Mystic Way in more complete and lovely terms.

Chapter 9

Puritans Against Arminians

One of the joys in reading *Four Quartets* is encountering a number of seventeenth-century Englishmen who I would probably never have met were it not for these poems. "Met" in the sense of learning about who they were and how their stories were used by Eliot to enrich the Quartets. For example, King Charles I, Nicholas Ferrar, William Laud, and Lancelot Andrewes were previously unknown to me. It has been a meaningful discovery of some English history of the early seventeenth century. More than the poetry itself, *Four Quartets*, especially "Little Gidding," provides a history lesson as well. This chapter will explore that history, providing one more reason to read the Quartets.

The seventeenth century in England opens with the death of the Tudor Queen, Elizabeth I (who had reigned for forty-four years), and the ascension of James Stuart, the son of Mary Stuart (1542–1587, who had been executed on Elizabeth's orders and whose dying words are quoted in the final line of "East Coker"— "In my end is my beginning") to the English throne in 1603. James added the title of James I of England to his title as James VI of Scots. During his reign, which lasted until 1625, the King James translation (Lancelot Andrewes was one of the translators) of the Bible was published.

At the death of James, his son Charles became king. The Stuarts had a strong belief in the Divine Right of Kings (by which they were answerable to God only and not to men) and thus were in constant conflict with the English Parliament. Father and son considered it a nuisance and an infringement on their kingly prerogatives to have to deal with Parliament at all. While all was relatively peaceful during James' reign, Charles had many conflicts with Parliament over taxes and religion. Parliament would not vote the taxes which Charles demanded so he dissolved Parliament and raised revenue in ways that did not require consent of Parliament.

The religious problem stemmed from the conflict between two groups vying to dictate the reformation of worship in the English Church. Puritans (or Calvinists) wished to eliminate all aspects of religious life associated with the Church of Rome. Moreover, the Puritans believed that God had chosen an elect for salvation (predestination). In contrast, Arminians (high church Anglicans) under the leadership of Archbishop William Laud (1573-1645) believed that free will had a role in salvation as well as observing the liturgy and sacraments.

Much of the dispute centered on the role of the church building itself. Puritans viewed the building as being a plain structure centered on preaching. For Laud, the church should be beautiful and holy, a place for formal prayer, ritual, and sacraments. Puritans regarded the Church of Rome as espousing false religion, while Arminians did not. There were angry disputes over what the clergy should wear and where the altar should be placed; even what the altar should be named (communion table or altar).

Charles was a strong supporter of Laud, having appointed him as Archbishop of Canterbury in 1633. The Puritans charged that Laud and Charles were really Papists. It did not help the dispute that Charles was married to Henrietta-Maria, who was a Roman Catholic and very publicly practiced her religion in London. Laud was a strong enforcer of Arminianism, having been strongly influenced in his position by Lancelot Andrewes (1555-1626), Bishop of Winchester. Eliot writes in his 1926 essay "Lancelot Andrewes" that Andrewes' devotion to public ritual was "bequeathed to William Laud."[1] Andrewes began his ministry under Queen Elizabeth at a time when Puritans were advocating that the English Church be modeled in the form of the church in Geneva, Switzerland. The Puritans wanted to discard bishops and their cathedrals, the *Book of Common Prayer*, and certain sacraments. During her reign, Elizabeth thwarted such changes. Andrewes, as chaplain to both Elizabeth and later James I, was a strong voice for retaining the more Catholic aspects of the English Church.

Andrewes was a great preacher whom Eliot calls "the first great preacher of the English Catholic Church"[2] and "second to none in the history of the formation of the English Church."[3] Even though Andrewes's sermons are little read today, Eliot found them to "rank with the finest prose of their time, of any time."[4] Eliot in his essay "Lancelot Andrewes" calls particular attention to the Christmas Day sermons Andrewes preached before King James between 1605 and 1624. These sermons all focus on the same subject, the Incarnation, which was to Andrewes an essential dogma. Eliot begins his first *Ariel Poem*, "Journey of the Magi," by selectively quoting from five lines in Andrews' 1622 Christmas sermon:

> A cold coming we had of it,
> Just the worst time of the year
> For a journey and such a long journey:
> The ways deep and the weather sharp,
> The very dead of winter.[5]

Eliot loosely quoted what Andrewes had written:

> A cold coming they had of it at this time of
> the year, just the worst time of the year to take
> a journey, and specially a long journey in.
> The ways deep, the weather sharp, the

1. Eliot, *For Lancelot Andrewes*, 18.
2. Ibid., 15.
3. Ibid., 26.
4. Ibid., 11.
5. Eliot, *Collected Poems*, 81.

days short, the sun farthest off, in solstitio
brumali, the very dead of winter.[6]

Andrewes's sermons emphasizing the Incarnation may have been the inspiration for Eliot to place the Incarnation at the center of the Quartets and other poems (see discussion in chapter 4).

The next interesting Englishman to consider is George Herbert. In spite of a thirty-five-year difference in their ages, Andrewes and Herbert were friends. Herbert was a devoted churchman in the style of Andrewes and rejected the Puritan position as well. At an early age Herbert showed great promise as a poet. While studying at Cambridge he was named public orator, probably due to his poetic skill. He hoped to rise to a high position in politics under the patronage of King James, but the King died in 1625, leaving Herbert without a patron to further his advancement in civic affairs. Herbert turned away from a life in politics in 1626 and became a priest and rector in the small village of Bemerton. Between 1630 and 1633 he wrote devotional poetry which was highly praised by Eliot. Early on Eliot did not consider Herbert to be an important poet, but later changed his mind and called him a "major poet," that is, a poet whose entire body of work is worthy to be read. On his deathbed he entrusted the manuscript of his poems to his good friend, Nicholas Ferrar, who saw to it that the poems were later published as *The Temple* which became the equivalent of a bestseller in the seventeenth century.

A coping strategy, albeit not common, for dealing with the contentious life of conflict between king and Parliament and between factions in the church was to simply withdraw from active life, much like going to live in a monastery. In 1626, both Ferrar and Herbert did exactly that—Herbert to Bemerton, and Ferrar to Little Gidding.

Central to Ferrar's story is his family's involvement with the Virginia Company, which in 1609 was granted a royal charter giving it exclusive control over the development of a colony in North

6. Andrewes, "Sermons of the Nativity Preached Upon Christmas-Day, 1622," lines 190–93.

America. The founding of Jamestown, Virginia occurred later that year. Nicholas's father was a leading official in the company until his advancing age prompted his replacement by Nicholas's older brother, John, and then later by Nicholas himself in 1622. It was not a propitious time for the company due to the colony's poor economic performance and a massacre of 357 colonists by Indians in 1622. Two years later the King withdrew his support for the private company and instead made Virginia a "royal" colony under the King's direct control. With the dissolution of the Virginia Company Nicholas entered what his principle biographer calls his "years of renunciation." Nicholas decided to withdraw from public life and create a community which fused a monastic style of life with the daily life of a parish composed of families.

He learned that a tiny hamlet in Huntingdonshire was for sale. He visited the place and discovered a large manor house and nearby a little church which had been converted into a hay barn. Both structures were in need of significant repairs. The hamlet was so insignificant that it was not shown on any maps of the area. Due to its isolation, it was just the place for Nicholas to establish the community he had in mind. The property was purchased in 1626 and he made preparations to move from London to Little Gidding.

Nicholas shared his decision to retire from active life and form a household dedicated to prayer with his family—his mother, Mary, his elder brother, John, his wife, Bathsheba, his sister, Susanna Collet, and her family. All decided to join Nicholas in moving from London to Little Gidding. There they adopted a way of living including saying the daily offices—Matins, the Litany and Evensong—and daily reading the entire Psalter. In order for Nicholas to officiate at these services, he was ordained deacon by Bishop Laud in 1626. In spite of ordination by Bishop Laud and the Ferrars' inclination to the high church position, they freely adopted certain Puritan practices as they saw fit, e.g., an emphasis on daily scripture reading and placing the communion table in the midst of the congregation instead of against the east wall. Their practice was not intended to be monastic—no vows of poverty, chastity, and obedience were taken—but instead was simply a family as a family choosing to live a life of prayer according to the *Book of Common Prayer*. Nicholas only lived until 1637. Thereafter, brother John and sister Susanna carried on the practices Nicholas had established until their deaths in 1657. The old practice of family daily prayer was then abandoned and Little Gidding reverted to simply being a farm until revived as a religious community two and a half centuries later.

Disputes between king and Parliament over fiscal and church affairs intensified in the 1630s. Because Parliament refused to authorize certain taxes, Charles chose to raise revenues on his own without legislative approval. On the advice of Laud in 1636, Charles commanded that the Scottish Church use a prayer book for worship which was based on the English *Book of Common Prayer*. The Scots reacted violently and adopted a covenant to uphold the Scottish kirk as it was without Charles' demand that Laudian practice be followed. Seventeenth-century English and Scots took their religion very seriously and were willing to resort to violence to defend their respective positions. The Bishops' Wars of 1639–1640 were the result. To impose his will on the Scots, Charles raised an army to invade Scotland. Doubling back on the revenue problem, Charles faced great difficulty in paying for his military forces because Parliament refused to vote the necessary funds. In 1640, a Scottish force invaded England and occupied much of the northern part of the country (as far south as Yorkshire). Parliament came under pressure from the occupation to act against what the king's opponents labeled "popery" and "royal tyranny." Because the doctrine of the Divine Right of Kings held that the "king could do no wrong," Parliament could not challenge the king directly, but instead chose to attack the king's close advisors, proxies for the king: the Earl of Strafford and Archbishop Laud. Both men had tried to assert the authority of the king—Strafford over Parliament and Laud over the church.

Thomas Wentworth, Earl of Strafford (1593–1641), was a leading advisor to the king and worked to consolidate the sovereign power of the king over Parliament. As lord deputy of Ireland beginning in 1633, he set about trying as well to establish royal authority in Ireland. He was recalled to England in 1639 to lead the army going north to subdue the Scottish revolt over the prayer book. Strafford failed to defeat the Scots and was recalled to England. He was arrested and impeached for treason. At trial there was scant evidence of treason presented, so Parliament changed tactics and instead passed a bill of attainder (a legislative sentence of guilt which required only suspicious evidence rather than a judicial process requiring a much higher level of proof in order to convict) imposing a death sentence. Charles was deeply upset by the verdict and initially refused to consent to the sentence. Strafford, however, wrote to the king urging him to sign the bill: "So now to set Your Majesties Conscience at liberty, I do most humbly beseech Your Majesty for prevention of evils, which may happen by Your refusal, to pass the Bill."[7] Strafford was willing to be a martyr to protect the king. Charles did sign the bill and Strafford was executed May 12, 1641.

Laud was a close ally of both the king and Strafford. Laud was arrested at the same time as Strafford and held in the Tower of London, but was not tried until 1644. Just as in the Strafford trial, Parliament was not able to produce convincing evidence that Laud had committed treason. Once again Parliament adopted a bill of attainder and imposed the death sentence on Laud. He was executed January 10, 1645.

The English Civil War or what one Roundhead described as "a war without an enemy" began in the summer of 1642. Roundhead Sir William Waller wrote to his Cavalier friend, Sir Ralph Hopton: "That Great God Who is the searcher of all hearts knows with what a sad fear I go upon this service, and with what a perfect hate I look upon a war without an enemy."[8] The war was father against son, brother against brother, resulting in the fracturing of families and friends. This war was not a conflict between different races, nationalities, or religions—although superficially it might appear to be the latter. While the Presbyterian Roundheads opposed the Anglican Cavaliers, both were strongly opposed to Roman Catholicism. Both sides had so much in common and in their view fought for the liberty

7. Burke, *Dictionary of the Peerages*, 567.
8. Gardiner, *1642–1644*, 168.

and salvation of the country. Their differences laid in whether Parliament or the monarch would be the ultimate authority. In addition to the two warring sides, there was a large third group who felt no strong sympathy for either Parliament or king; they hoped differences could be reconciled and the country could live in peace. Over time, however, it was impossible to remain neutral and uncommitted. Those who felt no sympathy for either side were forced to take sides as the warring parties seized towns, strongpoints, and military stores throughout the country; to hesitate in choosing a side could result in maltreatment by both sides.

The Royalists were most powerful in the west of England, Wales, and Cornwall; Parliament held London and eastern England. Over the course of three years there were a number of large, set battles—Edge Hill (1642), Roundway Down (1643), and Newbury (1643). More typical, however, than the large battles were hundreds of small skirmishes. In 1644, a Scottish army joined Parliamentary forces and helped win a major victory at Marston Moor. As a result Cromwell's forces were left in control of much of northern England. He reorganized his forces to create the "New Model Army" which on June 14, 1645, defeated the king at Naseby. This victory effectively ended the war due to the utter collapse of the king's army.

It was following the defeat of his army at Naseby that Charles ("broken king" and "king at nightfall") sought sanctuary at Little Gidding. Charles had previously visited the community (in 1633 and 1642) so knew it to be sympathetic to the royalist cause. John Ferrar, who then led the community following the death of Nicholas, feared that parliamentary troops might search for the king there and instead led him to a house miles away. According to some accounts, within a short period of time, in reprisal for harboring the king, Puritan troops ransacked and looted the church and its furnishings.

Following Naseby, Charles returned to Oxford where he had established his court after fleeing London in 1642. He remained in Oxford until he left in disguise (short hair and beard) in April 1646 hoping to avoid capture by Parliamentary forces which he successfully did for awhile. Eventually he surrendered to Scottish forces which were occupying parts of England. In 1647, Scottish forces withdrew from England and handed over Charles to Parliamentary forces. By November of that year Charles had managed to escape once again, but in short order was interned on the Isle of Wight. He was finally arrested in December 1648 and charged with "all the treasons, murders, ravages, burnings, spoils, desolations, damages and mischiefs to this nation."[9] He was promptly tried by a special court of army officers and members of Parliament and found guilty. He was beheaded on January 30, 1649.

The final person to deal with is John Milton (1608–74). He was an active polemicist during the Civil War and wrote in favor of Parliament and against the king. In addition he was a great poet whose principal works are *Paradise Lost* and *Samson Agonistes*. Since all the other men discussed in this chapter were fierce royalists, why would Eliot include an anti-royalist "who died blind and quiet" in the poem? A possible explanation is that Charles's influence did not stop with his death. Within weeks of his death a book of Charles's meditations, prayers, and his speech on the scaffold, known as *The King's Book* (*Eikon Basilike*), was circulating to great acclaim. The work was his spiritual legacy which sought to make Charles a martyr for the Church of England (like his grandmother Mary Stuart). The anti-royalist opposition sought to undercut the impact of the book by having Milton write a piece attacking *The King's Book*. Thus, Milton too is tied to the royalist cause even if the connection is an attack on that point of view. We must never forget that Eliot described himself as a "royalist in politics" (along with being an Anglo-Catholic in religion and a classicist in literature), so including a leading anti-royalist does bear some relationship to the martyr king.

With a better understanding of the history of the seventeenth century, identification of the allusions in "Little Gidding" can be suggested. In section I of the poem the physical place of Little Gidding is described:

> If you came at night like a broken king
> [Charles I following defeat at the Battle
> of Naseby in 1645]

9. Wedgewood, *A Coffin for King Charles*, 149.

If you came by day not knowing what you
    came for,
It would be the same, when you leave the
    rough road
And turn behind the pig-sty to the dull
    façade [of the small chapel which is
    still there today]
And the tombstone. [crypt of Nicholas Ferrar][10]

Then in section III of the poem many of the persons discussed earlier in this chapter become characters in the poem itself:

If I think, again, of this place [Little Gidding],
And of people, not wholly commendable,
    [possibly John Ferrar's wife, Bathsheba,
    who resented Nicholas and hated the
    pious way of life in the community]
Of no immediate kin or kindness,
But some of peculiar genius [possibly
    George Herbert],
All touched by a common genius
    [Nicholas Ferrar]
United in the strife which divided them
    [these persons were all royalists
    in the English Civil War],
If I think of a king at nightfall [Charles I again
    as he was fleeing the Naseby battlefield],
Of three men, and more, on the scaffold [Laud,
    Strafford, and Charles I]
And a few who died forgotten
In other places, here and abroad,
And of one who died blind and quiet
    [John Milton][11]

10. Eliot, *Collected Poems*, 201.
11. Ibid., 206.

Chapter 10

Lent

It was not until I learned from the widow of a recently departed friend that he had made a practice of reading *Four Quartets* daily during Lent each year that I gave any thought to the structure of the poems providing a perfect Lenten reading. There are four poems, each with five sections which are each divided into two subsections (as described below—the text does not facially indicate division into subsections). Do the math—four times five times two equals forty. Very neatly, there is a reading for each of the forty days in Lent.

The five sections of each of the quartets are delineated by a Roman numeral. Each section contains both an "a" and a "b" subsection. These subsections are not noted by the author in the text, but once we accept the idea that an "a" section deals with a temporal aspect, that is a worldly comment, whereas a "b" section deals with a timeless or divine topic, each section can easily be divided between an "a" and a "b."

In what follows the poems will be referred to in shorthand as follows: BN ("Burnt Norton"), EC ("East Coker"), DS ("The Dry Salvages"), and LG ("Little Gidding"). Thus, the very first section of "Burnt Norton" will be referred to as BN (I). The first subsection of BN (I) will be referred to as BN (Ia).

Therefore, a Lenten reading of *Four Quartets* could proceed in forty daily readings as follows:

Day 1: BN (Ia) (lines 1–16, beginning "Time present and time past"); prose statement asserting that past, present, and future are contained in a single dimension of time.

Day 2: BN (Ib) (lines 17–46, beginning "Other echoes"); an account of a brief experience out of time, hence in the eternal or vertical dimension (see chapter 4, Divine Geometry).

Day 3: BN (IIa) (lines 1–15, beginning "Garlic and sapphires in the mud"); a series of poetic images suggesting that nature and life itself are in flux, but yet there is a pattern.

Day 4: BN (IIb) (lines 16–43, beginning "At the still point of the turning world"); first mention of the "still point" which is where the pattern is apprehended and the divine encountered.

Day 5: BN (IIIa) (lines 1–24, beginning "Here is a place of disaffection"); the London subway, which is a symbol of temporal existence without meaning.

Day 6: BN (IIIb) (lines 25–37, beginning "Descend lower, descend only"); there is another place of darkness ("The Dark Night of the Soul" which leads to finding meaning in life).

Day 7: BN (IVa) (lines 1–5, beginning "Time and the bell have buried the day"); twilight of a different kind than BN-IIIa in a natural setting where there is an expectation of being touched.

Day 8: BN (IVb) (lines 6–10, beginning "Chill"); in spite of death (the yew tree is a symbol of death) the still point is always present.

Day 9: BN (Va) (lines 1–22, beginning "Words move, music moves"); writing, music, and art can reach into stillness "by the form, the pattern" and thus be incarnated.

Day 10: BN (Vb) (lines 23–39, beginning "The detail of the pattern is movement"); the eternal (Divine) touches the temporal as for example the experience in the rose garden and that experience is "here, now, always" available.

Day 11: EC (Ia) (lines 1–23, beginning "In my beginning is my end"); a riff on Ecclesiastes 3:1–8 ("to everthing there is a season . . . ")

Day 12: EC (Ib) (lines 24–50, beginning "In that open field"); adapts the proposition in EC(Ia) to a vision out of history in which a married couple dances around a bonfire.

Day 13: EC (IIa) (lines 1–17, beginning "What is the late November doing"); nature is disturbed—flowers are not blooming in the natural order and the constellations are in chaos.

Day 14: EC (IIb) (lines 18–50, beginning "That was a way of putting it"); there is chaos in the life of an individual which is not resolved by the "wisdom of age;" humility is the only wisdom which can be hoped for.

Day 15: EC (IIIa) (lines 1–23, beginning "O dark, dark, dark"); human life is transitory and ends in darkness like in a theatre as the scenery is changed or when a subway train stops between stations or the mind is under anesthesia.

Day 16: EC (IIIb) (lines 24–45, beginning "I said to my soul"); if we are quiet, still, and follow the Via Negativa, we can wait for a different kind of darkness, the darkness of God.

Day 17: EC (IVa) (lines 1–15, beginning "The wounded surgeon plies the steel"); man is sick but health can be restored only if "our sickness must grow worse."

Day 18: EC (IVb) (lines 16–25, beginning "The chill ascends from feet to knees"); Eucharist makes us well again.

Day 19: EC (Va) (lines 1–18, beginning "So here I am"): similar to cycles described earlier in EC, there is a cycle to literary work as well.

Day 20: EC (Vb) (llines 19–38, beginning "Home is where one starts from;" we must be explorers by being "still and still moving" in order to move into another intensity, a deeper communion or union with God. [Note: This is the prelude to DS in the references to the sea and its creatures in lines 37–38.].

Day 21: DS (Ia) (lines 1–24, beginning "I do not know much about gods"); human time (symbolized by the "river") is juxtaposed to the time older that human time (symbolized by the "sea").

Day 22: DS (Ib) (lines 25–48, beginning "The sea has many voices"); the sea has many voices, but the most significant is the "tolling bell" which reminds us of "a time / Older than the time of chronometers" (e.g., eternity).

Day 23: DS (IIa) (lines 1–36, beginning "Where is there an end of it"); meaning and value in one life is not found in past or future, but only in the Annunciation (e.g., the announcement that the Divine would be in the world).

Day 24: DS (IIb) (lines 37–75, beginning "It seems, as one becomes older"); in our past there are both moments of "sudden illumination" and moments of agony (which are more easily seen in the lives of others), but there is always "the ragged rock in restless waters" (metaphor for incarnation, see chapter 3).

Day 25: DS (IIIa) (lines 1–22, beginning "I sometimes wonder if that is what Krishna meant"); the past cannot be escaped by looking to the future because we are not the same person now who experienced the past and, moreover, "the past is not finished" (William Faulkner wrote "The past is not dead, it is not even past.")

Day 26: DS (IIIb) (lines 23–45, beginning "At nightfall, in the rigging and the aerial"); words from the *Bhagavad Gita* encouraging us to act not with the thought of "the fruits of action," but according to the role assigned to each in life.

Day 27: DS (IVa) (lines 1–10, beginning "Lady whose shrine stands on the promontory"); prayer to Blessed Virgin Mother to protect seamen and their families.

Day 28: DS (IVb) (lines 11–15, beginning "Also pray for those who were in ships"); The prayer is expanded to include other sailors as well as others who are not within hearing of the "sea's bell" which calls to a perpetual angelus (a prayer in the Roman Catholic Church in commemoration of the Incarnation).

Day 29: DS (Va) (lines 1–17, beginning "To communicate with Mars"); listing of various methods man has used to try to predict the future, i.e., horoscope, haruspicate (examine animal intestines), scry (crystal gazing), handwriting analysis, palm reading, sortilege (casting lots), tarot cards, pentagram, barbituric acid (hypnotic drug), and psychoanalysis.

Day 30: DS (Vb) (lines 18–50, beginning "But to apprehend"); the climax of the Quartets is apprehension of incarnation, "point of intersection of the timeless / With time"; whereas a saint through a lifetime of love apprehends the intersection, the rest of mankind experiences only "hints and guesses."

Day 31: LG (Ia) (lines 1–19, beginning "Midwinter spring is its own season"); on occasion during winter ("dark time of the year") there will be a spring-like day ("spring time / But not in time's covenant").

Day 32: LG (Ib) (lines 20–53, beginning "If you came this way"); the poet imagines a visit to Little Gidding, a remote village in Huntingdonshire, where a religious community based on the family was established in 1626 by Nicholas Ferrar. The community was destroyed in 1647 by Cromwell's army during the English Civil War. A small chapel was restored in the nineteenth century. Nevertheless, it is not clear whether the visit occurs in the present, or in the past when "a broken king" (Charles I following his defeat at the battle of Naseby) visited in 1645. Little Gidding is one of those special places at the "world's end" where the intersection of time and eternity is easily perceived. There are other such places, outside of England, such as Iona ("the sea jaws"), Glendalough ("dark lake"), Thebaid ("desert"), and Padua ("city").

Day 33: LG (IIa) (lines 1–24, beginning "Ash on an old man's sleeve"); death and destruction of the four elements (air, earth, water, and fire).

Day 34: LG (IIb) (lines 25–96, beginning "In the uncertain hour before the morning"); homage to Dante's *Inferno* in which the London Blitz is compared to Dante's visit to the underworld and the poet meets "a familiar compound ghost."

Day 35: LG (IIIa) (lines 1–16, beginning "There are three conditions"); there are three conditions which may look alike, but are different—attachment, detachment, and indifference.

Day 36: LG (IIIb) (lines 17–50, beginning "Sin is Behovely [inevitable];" begins with a quotation from Dame Julian of Norwich ("Sin is Behovely, but / All shall be well, and / All manner of thing shall be well) and then the poem returns to a vision of Little Gidding and certain seventeenth-century persons with an association with Little Gidding or the English Civil War, e.g., Nicholas

Farrer ("peculiar genius"), his sister-in-law, Bathsheba ("not wholly commendable"), Charles I ("a king at nightfall"), Archbishop Laud and Earl of Strafford ("three men and more on the scaffold"), and John Milton ("one who died blind").

Day 37: LG (IVa) (lines 1–7, beginning "The dove descending breaks the air"); the dove is a German bomber bringing death, but hope lies in redemption by the fire of the Holy Spirit.

Day 38: LG (IVb) (lines 8–14, beginning "Who then devised the torment?"); human suffering is a manifestation of God's love (George Herbert, see chapter 9) and man will be consumed by the fire of the German bomber or the fire of the Holy Spirit.

Day 39: LG (Va) (lines 1–24, beginning "What we call the beginning is often the end"); beginning (birth) and end (death) are the same. History has meaning only because it contains "a pattern / Of timeless moments".

Day 40: LG (Vb) (lines 25–46, beginning "With the drawing of this love [quote from *The Cloud of Unknowing*—"What weary wretched heart and sleeping in sloth is that, the which is not wakened with the drawing of this love and the voice of this calling?"];" after exploring we shall arrive where we started, and will "know the place for the first time." At this point the poem recapitulates several of the images from earlier Quartets, e.g., earth (EC), the longest river (DS), children (BN), and stillness. "And the fire and the rose are one." This final line has been the subject of speculation as to Eliot's intended meaning. Let me offer an interpretation: The first encounter with the divine (eternity) occurs in the rose garden in "Burnt Norton." The "crowned knot of fire" (see *The Cloud of Unknowing*—"knit the ghostly knot of burning love betwixt thee and thy God") alludes to God's love. Thus, when God's love is joined with the experience in the rose garden that "condition of complete simplicity / (Costing not less that everything)" is realized. In Dantean terms, this is the Beatific Vision.

Chapter 11

Love Story

There is a final, very personal, reason for me to read *Four Quartets*. Soon after meeting Mary Lou, my wife, there was an immediate sign that there was going to be something special in our friendship.

Although we had attended the same grade school and high school in the 1960s, we had never met until a mutual friend introduced us in 2001. That introduction happened in Kansas City where I was living, and the very next weekend I had travel plans to Chicago where Mary Lou was living. I asked her to have dinner one evening. I arrived at her apartment with a small gift—a copy of *Four Quartets*, inscribed as follows: "These poems have been the source of much understanding, inspiration, and strength for me since 'discovering' them almost twenty years ago. I hope you will find value in them too." Her immediate response was, "You are not going to believe this." She took me to her study and pulled a book from the middle of a stack by a chair. The book was *T.S. Eliot: Collected Poems, 1909–1962*. The corner of one of the pages had been turned down, and there was yellow highlighting in "East Coker." She told me that just weeks earlier she had pulled this book off the stack in order to find a passage she wanted to re-read. Well, we looked at each other in utter amazement. We agreed that many have not heard of Eliot, but even among those who recognize the name, there are few who have ever read the Quartets. That shared love of the poems was a sign that our relationship was off to a great start—so much so that we were married later that year. At our wedding I read lines from "Little Gidding":

> We shall not cease from exploration
> And the end of all our exploring
> Will be to arrive where we started
> And know the place for the first time.[1]

For our fifth anniversary Mary Lou gave me a gold pocket-watch inscribed with these words from "East Coker"—"Love is most nearly itself / When here and now cease to matter."[2]

---

1. Eliot, *Collected Poems*, 208.
2. Ibid., 189.

Appendix

Four Quartets by T.S. Eliot

	Burnt Norton 1935	East Coker 1940	The Dry Salvages 1941	Little Gidding 1941-42
Place	Country house in Gloustershire, England visited by Eliot in 1934 with Emily Hale	Homestead of Eliot family before immigration to America in 17th century; visited by Eliot in 1936; Eliot is buried there	"A small group of rocks with a beacon off Massachusetts coast"; Eliot family vacationed nearby	Site of Anglican community established by Nicolas Ferrar in 1625; visited by Eliot in 1936
Element	Air	Earth	Water	Fire
Season	Spring (early summer)	Summer	Fall	Winter
Time	Personal time	Personal and social time Lifetime of man Succession of men's lifetimes	Universal history Cosmic time	Eternity (timeless)
Experience of the Divine	The moment	Man's opportunity of transforming himself to allow the divine to incarnate itself in his lifetime	Time and nature are alien, hostile	Experience outside of time
Dogma	Grace	Faith Atonement	Hope Incarnation	Love Pentecost
Divine person	God the creator	Christ	Virgin Mary	Holy Spirit

Purpose: "The experience of believing a dogma" - T.S. Eliot

Theme: Redemption of time through the Incarnation

Discovery: It is possible to know God and hence know immortality

Bibliography

Andrewes, Lancelot. "Sermons of the Nativity Preached Upon Christmas-Day, 1622."https://civilewriver.files.wordpress.com/2013/01/lancelot-andrewes -Christmas sermon-16222.pdf.

Atkins, G. Douglas. *Reading T. S. Eliot: Four Quartets and The Journey Towards Understanding.* New York: Palgrave Macmillan, 2012.

———. *T. S. Eliot and The Fulfillment of Christian Poetics.* New York: Palgrave Macmillan, 2014.

———. *T. S. Eliot and the Essay.* Waco, TX: Baylor University Press, 2010.

Augustine. *The Confessions of St. Augustine.* Translated by John K. Ryan. Garden City, NY: Image, 1960.

Barth, Karl. *The Epistle to the Romans.* New York: Oxford University Press, 1976.

Bhagavad Gita, The. Translated by Barbara Stoler Miller. New York: Bantam Dell, 2004.

Book of Common Prayer, The. New York: Church Publishing. 1979.

Burke, John-Bernard. A Genealogical and Heraldic Dictionary of the Peerages of England. London: Henry Colburn, 1846.

Cloud of Unknowing, The. Edited by William Johnston. New York: Image, 1973.

Dante. *The Divine Comedy.* Translated by Allen Mandelbaum. New York: Knopf, 1995.

Eliot, T. S. *Collected Poems,* 1909–1962. San Diego: Harcourt Brace Jovanovich, 1963.

———. *The Complete Poems and Plays,* 1909–1950. New York: Harcourt Brace, 1980.

———. *For Lancelot Andrewes.* London: Faber and Faber, 1970.

———. *The Sacred Wood and Major Early Essays.* Mineola, NY: Dover, 1998.

———. *Selected Essays.* London: Faber and Faber, 1999.

————. *To Criticize the Critic and Other Writings.* Lincoln: University of Nebraska Press, 1991.

————. "Yeats." http://www.tseliot.com/essays/yeats.

Eliot, Valerie and John Haffenden, eds. *The Letters of T. S. Eliot,* Volume 3, 1926–1927. New Haven, CT: Yale University Press, 2012.

————. *The Letters of T. S. Eliot,* Volume 4, 1928–1929. New Haven, CT: Yale University Press, 2013.

————. *The Letters of T. S. Eliot,* Volume 5, 1930–1931. London: Faber and Faber, 2014.

————. *The Letters of T. S. Eliot,* Volume 6, 1932–1933. London: Faber and Faber, 2016.

Gardiner, Samuel Rawson. 1642–1644. London: Longmans, Green, 1894.

Gordon, Lyndall. *T. S. Eliot: An Imperfect Life.* New York: W. W. Norton, 1999.

Herbert, George. *The Complete English Works.* Edited by Ann Pasternak Slater. New York: Alfred A. Knopf, 1995.

John of the Cross. *The Collected Works of St. John of the Cross.* Translated by Kieran Kavanaugh and Otilio Rodreguez. Washington, DC: ICS, 1973.

Johnston, William. *The Still Point: Reflections on Zen and Christian Mysticism.* New York: Harper and Row, 1970.

Julian of Norwich. *Revelations of Divine Love.* Translated by Clifton Wolters. New York: Penguin, 1966.

Kelsey, Morton. *The Other Side of Silence.* New York: Paulist, 1997.

Lobb, Edward, ed. *Words in Time.* Ann Arbor: The University of Michigan Press. 1993.

Maycock, A. L. *Nicholas Ferrar of Little Gidding.* Grand Rapids, MI: W. B. Eerdmans, 1980.

Menard, Louis. "Practical Cat." *The New Yorker* (2011). www.newyorker.com/magazine/2011/09/19/practical-cat.

Raine, Craig. *T. S. Eliot.* New York: Oxford University Press, 2006.

Ravindea, Ravi. *The Pilgrim Soul.* Wheaton, IL: Theosophical, 2014.

Ricks, Christopher and Jim McCue, eds. *The Poems of T. S. Eliot, Vol. 1.* Baltimore: Johns Hopkins University Press, 2015.

Shakespeare, William. *The Riverside Shakespeare.* 2nd ed. Boston: Houghton Mifflin, 1997.

Shannon, William H. *Thomas Merton's Dark Path.* New York: Penguin, 1982.

Spurr, Barry. *Anglo-Catholic in Religion: T. S. Eliot and Christianity.* Cambridge: Lutterworth, 2010.

Tillich, Paul. *The New Being.* Lincoln: University of Nebraska Press, 2005.

Tombs, Robert. *The English and Their History.* New York: Alfred A. Knopf, 2015.

Underhill, Evelyn. *Mysticism: A Study in the Nature and Development of Man's Spiritual Consciousness.* Mineola, NY: Dover, 2002.

Webster's New World College Dictionary, 5th ed. New York: Houghton Mifflin Harcourt, 2014.

Wedgewood, C. V. *A Coffin for King Charles.* New York: Macmillan, 1964.

Printed in Great Britain
by Amazon